WOMAN
FIRST AMONG
THE FAITHFUL

WOMAN
FIRST AMONG
THE FAITHFUL

Francis J. Moloney, SDB

INTRODUCTION BY THOMAS H. GREEN, SJ

AVE MARIA PRESS
Notre Dame, Indiana 46556

Originally published by Dove Communications, Australia.
Copyright © 1984 Francis J. Moloney, S.D.B.

Published in the United States by Ave Maria Press.
© Copyright 1986 Francis J. Moloney, S.D.B.

Library of Congress Catalog Card Number: 85-73197

International Standard Book Number: 0-87793-332-4
                                      0-87793-333-2 (pbk.)

Cover design: Elizabeth J. French

Printed and bound in the United States of America.

For one who, through her gentleness,
faith and openness to God's ways
is a constant source of joy and
encouragement to me

CONTENTS

INTRODUCTION

Thomas H. Green, S. J.

About a year after an earlier and much shorter version of the present study (entitled *Woman in the New Testament*) appeared in Australia in 1981, I received a copy from an Australian sister-friend of mine. She was enthusiastic about the book and, knowing my interest in the entry of women into a fuller participation in the ministerial life of the Church, she thought that I would be enthusiastic too. She was right. The author, Francis J. Moloney, SDB, had, as a respected exegete, attempted a serious, balanced exploration of the New Testament evidence concerning the place of women in the life and ministry of Jesus and of the early Church. This was neither a tract nor a diatribe. While Father Moloney brought much feeling to the question — and made no attempt to conceal his sympathy for the basic thrust of the women's movement in the Church — he desired only to let the Scripture reveal its own truth on the matter. It was no mean challenge: to maintain exegetical rigor in discussing a question about which feelings today (including his own) run strong.

I felt he succeeded admirably, though the book was brief and certain parts of the New Testament came in for only passing notice at best. His sections on woman in Luke and in John's gospel were the longest and strongest. The section on Paul, while much shorter, was particularly striking because of the fresh perspective he provided — a considerable change from the traditional anti-feminist picture of Paul. For this reason, I suggested to the Daughters of St. Paul that they consider reprinting *Woman in the New Testament* for Filipino readers. In some important ways our situation is very different from that of Australia or the United States: our society is strongly matriarchal, despite a confusing and misleading veneer of male dominance. Generally much more is demanded of girls from their earliest years, with the result that they tend to be stronger and more responsible as they mature. But we too fall far short of the freedom of spirit, the at-homeness with our sexual identity and that of others, which Father Moloney finds to be such a striking quality of Jesus of Nazareth. I felt that the scriptural vision of woman had as much to teach us as anyone in the 'West'.

Because the Daughters of St. Paul agreed, they contacted Fr.

Moloney and proposed reprinting his book in Manila. In reply he pointed out that the 'book' in question was really the text of two lectures given to a group of Australian sisters in 1980. Rather than allow the reprinting of these two lectures, he sent them the draft of an expanded version on which he had already been working. This version, which appeared in Manila in 1984, again as *Woman in the New Testament*, was soon followed by a slightly revised and amplified Australian version, *Woman: First Among the Faithful*.

I mention the history of the evolution of the present text to underscore the care and exacting scholarship which have gone into it. Fr. Moloney tells us in the Preface that it is still not 'exhaustive', but that it does 'offer an interpretation of the major woman-texts found through (the New Testament) traditions' (page 11). I believe, that Luke and John present a strong and positive picture of the role of women in the redemptive life of Jesus. But it is a surprise, and a joy, to discover that Matthew and Paul — once we consider them in the context of their time and culture — also represent a significant advance beyond then-prevalent attitudes. Best of all, for me, is the realization that the attitudes and values of Jesus Himself are at the root of this new vision.

As in other areas of development of doctrine, Jesus' full revelation has been absorbed only slowly and haltingly into the consciousness of the Church. Apostolic spirituality, for example, took more than a millenium to grasp clearly the integration of contemplation and action revealed in the life of Jesus Himself. The process, in fact, is still incomplete, as the writings of the best of the liberation theologians make clear. Similarly, the full Christic meaning of the beautiful Judaic metaphor, 'the people of God', is only now coming into prominence in our ecclesial consciousness.

Is this slow and often erratic assimilation of the full riches of Jesus' revelation a reason to waver in faith or to turn away from the Church in anger? I don't think so; not at least if we understand the fundamental dynamic of the development of doctrine. Perhaps I have been blessed: my doctoral thesis was on the philosophy of evolution — an experience which has given me a deeper and richer sense of the slow, seemingly random way in which God works in creation and in history. As St. Thomas Aquinas pointed out long ago, God normally works through natural causes. He respects the laws (His laws) of His creation and the freedom (His gift) of His human creatures. We are frustrated by the slowness and the groping, but I doubt that He is: our vision is limited by a life-span of seventy years, but His is unimaginably longer. In lecturing, I try to convey something of this divine, evolutionary, long-range perspective as follows: 500,000 years from now, when a Church historian is lecturing to a class of

9

men and women preparing for ordination, I expect that Vatican II will be considered part of *early* Church history. He (she) may well say: 'Back in 1985, the post-Vatican II Church had problems and blind spots which are strange for us. But perhaps we should not be surprised. After all, they lived too close to the time of Jesus to have digested His words fully.'

Do I fully believe that the world and the Church will last that long, and that such a lecture may one day be given? Yes, I do. The long ages of preparation for the Messiah's coming (beginning, it appears, with the first 'big bang' from which our cosmos evolved) suggest, it seems to me, a comparably long time for the unfolding of the Kingdom He established. Indeed, it seems that such a perspective is necessary to make divine sense of our slow journey to Christian maturity — to give the Lord time to write straight with all our crooked lines.

It is from this perspective, too, that I hear Fr. Moloney tell us that there is still work to be done — that he has not yet explored all the relevant passages or sketched all the lines of the New Testament picture of woman. But the present book is a real step forward on the long journey. It makes its case convincingly: women are not only equal before God but they play a unique and significant role in the mystery of redemption. In fact, as I read, I felt that what may be needed now is a similar study of *man* in the New Testament! The men in Fr. Moloney's story don't always come across very sympathetically, by contrast with (and even as foils for) the women. But that in itself is, perhaps, a sign that he has done his job thoroughly and convincingly. The liberated women whom I have known and loved — from my earliest years and beginning with my own mother — clearly are heirs to a long and honorable biblical tradition. Their roots are in the New Testament Gospel of Jesus Christ.

Thomas H. Green, S.J.
San Jose Seminary
Manila, Philippines

PREFACE

'The voices of women' are now being heard in the Christian Churches.[1] This is an important testimony to the presence of the life of the Spirit in the Church, and it has led to an urgent need to reflect deeply upon the role and place of women in the whole Christian economy. Most of the significant work so far in this area has been done by the women themselves, and this is important.[2] The book that follows is an attempt on the part of a male biblical scholar to examine the sources of our faith and our tradition and to trace a New Testament theology of woman.

I am anxious that this book be seen as a challenge to both women and men, and I am also anxious that women read it as an important *male* contribution to a scholarly discipline where they have worked so hard — often with little support and even less understanding.[3] Yet, this is not 'a work of the heart'. There must be no compromising in a critical use of the techniques of contemporary New Testament scholarship. In the light of the strong recent return to the old securities of a fundamentalism that is so basic to a certain vision of the Church and her way in the world, I wish to go on questioning those so-called 'securities' through an honest appreciation of what the text meant for its original authors, readers and listeners. It is at that level that we can touch again the inspiring and inspired life of the early Church, and we can be challenged in our own time to be caught up into God's ways, rather than in the comfort of our own.

My method of approach is simple, and it can be grasped from a glance at the list of contents. I will move — more or less following the chronological development of the writings themselves — through the growing tradition of the early Church, as it is revealed in the pages of the New Testament: Jesus of Nazareth, Paul, Matthew, Luke, the Apocalypse, and finally, the Gospel of John. Although my analysis will not be exhaustive, I will offer an interpretation of the major woman-texts found through these traditions, attempting, in conclusion, to draw some theological and practical observations that arise from the New Testament itself.[4]

One further remark must be made at this stage. I have deliberately avoided any discussion of the issue of the ministry of women. This is

a thorny, and, in some places, a heated question with serious doc-
trinal and ecumenical implications. There can be little doubt that
women played an important ministerial role in the early Church,[5]
but it is equally clear that the New Testament authors were not
concerning themselves with any argument for or against such a
function. It is certainly useful and illuminating to investigate the
historical implications of particular texts, but one should not make
the mistake of then concluding: it was so in the early Church, and
therefore should also be so in the contemporary Church.[6] The matter
is much more complicated. We must not leap across the centuries
with the New Testament in hand. Apart from the obvious anachro-
nisms that such a practice would create in the life of the twentieth
century Church, it would be a sad return to the old 'proof text'
practice of the theological manuals that we nowadays so rightly
condemn.

I am sure that most of my readers are aware of the ever-increasing
volume of material available on the situation of women in the ancient world. Books and articles abound on women's sexual, social,
political and religious role in the ancient Near East, Egypt, Greece,
the Hellenistic world etc.[7] What follows is *not* a further contribution
to a study of 'woman in New Testament times'.[8] I am more interested in the use of the image of 'woman' in major theological contexts (such as Apocalypse 12, 17-18 and 21, and John 16, 21-24)
and the Gospels' consistent use of woman characters in narratives
that seem to be deliberately constructed to make important theological points, generally on the question of discipleship (such as Mark
5, 21-34; 12, 41-44; Luke 1-2; Matthew 1, 1-7; John 4, 7-30; 20,
1-2, 11-18). There is a *theological* use of 'woman' that needs to be
explored in its own right. Of course, the situation of women in the
time of Jesus and in the early Church is important background to
this theological use of women by the authors of the New Testament,
but the New Testament says much more about women than where
they stood in first-century social mores. Thus, this book is centered
upon the theological use of the women characters of the New Testament, and the important use of the image of 'the woman'.

Contemporary psychology has done us a great service in insisting
that women have not cornered the market on womanly qualities, just
as men have not done so with manly qualities. There are, fortunately,
male and female qualities in each one of us, be we woman or man.[9]
We must not be ashamed of this, and even though my analysis of the
New Testament material will present 'woman' in a certain light, the
challenge of this material is universal, so that we may all realize our
full potential as women and men of faith.

I have been thinking, writing and speaking on these matters in all

States of Australia and in New Zealand over the past four years. Everywhere I have met excitement and openness — sometimes a stimulating tough-mindedness — and always affection and real care. Above all, I have found that Religious women were prepared to travel long distances and to give up their few moments of respite from the ever-increasing burdens of their day-to-day apostolic involvement to listen carefully and critically to what was being discussed. There are often snide remarks passed among male members of the Church about the 'seminar sisters'. I can only comment on such remarks by saying that if faith is a journey away from our own securities, into the challenge of a future that only God can create, then the open-minded searching of these women and their hunger for solid understanding of the Word of God have indicated to me that the New Testament is, after all, correct: when it comes to faith, women, not men, lead the way. They are, indeed, 'first among the faithful'.

Francis J. Moloney, S.D.B.
Salesian Theological College
Oakleigh, Victoria , Australia

THE DISCUSSION

There is little need for me to indicate the importance of the subject of this book. We are all aware of a powerful interest in woman as such, highlighted in the 60s by the liberation movement, and since then steadily gaining a firmer footing as more serious study is given to all aspects of the person and role of woman in contemporary society. The literature devoted to these questions, although at times disturbingly strident, is immense, and even those devoting all their time and attention to this discipline must face a mammoth task in keeping in touch with it all.[1] What follows is purely a biblical reflection. As I have just mentioned, some of the contemporary writing, especially by women themselves, is sometimes strident. Whatever one might feel about the approach of some of our women authors and some of the more vocal women's movements, this stridency must be recognized as a genuine expression of a deeply felt frustration, and an expression of a righteous anger in a situation where distinctions and priorities are too rapidly and too neatly drawn on the basis of masculinity and femininity. The stridency, frustration and anger are, of course, justifiable and understandable, but often they are met with ridicule. In this way, the situation is only worsened, and the stridency intensified.

What we have experienced over the past few decades has been a gradual recognition and verbalizing of a simple fact: women were not made inferior, and therefore should not be treated as such. The Judeo-Christian tradition has been founded on such a belief. As far back as the ninth century BC the Jahwist had already indicated that there was to be a radical equality and mutuality between man and woman (Genesis 2, 18-25).[2] The inequality that is so much a part of our own scene was also part and parcel of the world of the Jahwist. However, he rightly saw that it could only be understood as the result of sin. The whole story of subordination and pain is told as a result of the sinful situation that has come into the lives of men and women because they have decided that they would prefer to do things their way, rather than God's way (Genesis 3, 14-19).[3] It is tragic that twenty-eight centuries later we are still quite happy to settle for such disorder in the relationships that exist between man and woman — and ridicule those who suggest that such a situation is wrong.

The biblical reflection that follows will be limited to the pages of the New Testament, and it is an attempt to look again at the word of God, to see if some light can be shed on how things *should* be. It is, therefore, a wholly positive approach to the question. Of course, it begins with a prejudice, which I hope most people who pick up this book will share with me: if we are to find an authoritative *starting point* for our reflections upon woman, then we must turn to the word of God. It will not provide *all* the answers, and for that reason I have stressed the words 'starting point'. The biblical literature is necessarily linked to the times, customs and situations that produced it. These elements vary considerably, even within the books of the Bible itself. Yet, despite all this, I believe that God has revealed himself and his plan for us in a once-and-for-all way in the 'messiness' of an incarnation, and in the 'messiness' of the limitations of human beings, their ideals, hopes and experiences, and their attempt to communicate these ideals, hopes and experiences through the poverty of a written word.[4] Despite the difficulties that a critical reading of the New Testament will always present, as it honestly assesses the conflicting experiences and evidence of the various traditions, it never ceases to amaze me that through it all there is a remarkable 'newness' and a never-ending set of questions that this all-too-human book keeps placing before me. Surely this was one of the major reasons why the early Church adopted these particular books as its authoritative 'New Testament' to be placed side by side with the 'Old Testament'. Precisely because our God speaks to us in this way, we, in the 'messiness' of our own situation, can hopefully turn to the word of the New Testament to find some indications of his plan and purpose.

In the midst of what is sometimes a very heated discussion, it appears to me that it is of immense value to approach the biblical material without any axes to grind. Perhaps one of the difficulties of some of the earlier studies in the area of theology of woman was the rigidity and certainty of authors on both sides of the debate; they all seemed to argue as if they had all the answers. This is no longer the case. The works of such scholars as Mary Daly, Elisabeth Schüssler Fiorenza, Sandra Schneiders, Monika Hellwig, Maria Boulding, Rosemary Ruether, Elisabeth Moltmann-Wendel and many others, show a wonderful sensitivity to the complexity of the theological problem.[5] The balance and skill of these scholars threaten their male counterparts less. More patience is still needed, as even the most attentive and searching male scholars are necessarily caught within a whole tradition of words and thought patterns that has grown over two thousand years of male dominance. This limitation will not be overcome without effort and patience from all concerned. Nevertheless there is every indication that the stage is now set for a more fruitful dialogue, and I would hope that this slight contribution on Woman in the New Testament will be of some help.

As I have already indicated in both the title of the book and in the Preface, I have deliberately limited my discussion to the theme of 'woman' in the New Testament, and not to 'women'. This means that I am not concerned with a study of all the women characters who appear in the pages of the New Testament; I am attempting to trace some overarching themes that touch upon 'woman' as such. Therefore, what follows will be necessarily selective, and I suppose that such a decision limits the significance of this contribution. However, in a theme so vast, some sort of control had to be exercised.

This limitation leads me to a further consequence. I will devote a lot of space to the most important 'woman' in the New Testament: the Mother of Jesus. There can be little doubt that for all the New Testament authors (*including* Paul — see Galatians 4, 4), for one reason or another, the Mother of Jesus was a most important 'woman'. This must not scare us off at the outset. Unfortunately, our idea of Mary, because of the undue influence of some 1500 years of tradition and the gradual exaltation of her person in that tradition, is now rather distant from the picture of Mary presented by the New Testament.[6] I believe that we have little to fear and a lot to learn from a serious presentation of the person of Mary as she is found in the pages of the New Testament. We will find that she is, first and foremost, a woman, a human being with whom women and men of all ages can and should identify themselves and their own experience of God's intervention in their lives. All contemporary Mariological studies are quick to recognize the 'discipleship' element in the New Testament's portrait of Mary.[7] This immediately lifts her out of any specifically sexual function. She challenges all of us to a radical following of the word and person of Jesus of Nazareth, cost what it may, be we male or female. Fortunately, as I have already mentioned, we are all *both* male and female, and thus the challenge of Mary is a challenge to wholeness. What makes Mary so important in a study of woman in the New Testament is precisely the recognition of the New Testament authors that through this woman God has chosen to act among us in a unique way, and the womanliness of Mary is essential to a correct understanding of God's action and her response to it.

Some readers will find that my analysis of the material is too brief. They are quite correct. Every single passage from the New Testament that I will be handling deserves a long, detailed and careful analysis.

Many of them have been the subject of considerable scholarly debate. We cannot delve into all of that, although I will try to refer readers to places where such an approach is available. I will often have to pass rapidly over a text, drawing conclusions after an all-too-brief analysis. I beg the readers' pardon and patience for such a procedure, assuring them that the major part of my conclusions here have come as the result of a long familiarity with the text and contemporary scholarship's evaluation of it. I trust that the soundness of the results may be the best proof of the soundness of my underlying method of approaching and interpreting these important passages.

As I have already mentioned, I lay no claim to have uncovered all the answers, but it appears to me that there is a remarkable unified presentation of the place and function of woman within the Christian view of things, even though the texts that we will examine come from a variety of authors writing at different times to different people in different places, all facing different pastoral problems. The Corinthian community addressed by Paul in the early 50s of the first century was not the audience addressed by John the Seer or John the Evangelist at the end of the same century. Yet there is a certain coherence that can be seen running from the teaching of Jesus, through Paul and the Evangelists, into the end of the century. I hope that what follows will show that this is the case, and that this message from the pages of the New Testament has something important to say to us today. Again, as I have already mentioned, what I have to say in the following pages is not the *end* of my research into this question, but the *beginning*.

JESUS OF NAZARETH

There are enormous difficulties involved in the rediscovery and correct interpretation of the nature of Jesus' personal relationships and his psychological attitudes. There have been several recent and varied attempts to do this in the area of Jesus' sexuality,[8] but it is widely admitted that the evidence is scarce, and that care must be taken not to make too many decisions on the basis of scant material. The accounts of the life of Jesus, as we have them in our four canonical Gospels, are heavily conditioned by each Evangelist's theological point of view, and many would argue that it is simply impossible to claim that we can glean any sort of portrait of Jesus' attitudes. In my opinion, this oft-repeated scepticism is too rapidly assumed. It is remarkable just how much material there is in the Gospels that gives us a rather startling vision of how Jesus related to women, and enables us to come closer to his attitude to woman as such.

Although this book is not dedicated to a detailed study of each relevant passage, it is valuable to see clearly how much material, coming from a wide variety of traditions, is dedicated to the question of Jesus and women. It is also quite probable that most of this material, which I will now list, can be traced back in one form or another to the life and experience of the historical Jesus.[9] The texts can be grouped in the following fashion.

1. *Women feature as the main protagonists in a series of miracle stories, all of which come from Mark's Gospel, originally, and have generally been retold by Matthew and Luke.*[10]
(a) The healing of Peter's mother-in-law (Mark 1, 29-31; Matthew 8, 14-15; Luke 4, 38-39).
(b) The healing of the woman with the hemorrhage (Mark 5, 24-34; Matthew 9, 20-22; Luke 8, 43-48).
(c) The raising of the daughter of Jairus (Mark 5, 21-24, 35-43).
(d) The Syrophoenician woman (Mark 7, 24-30; Matthew 15, 21-28).
2. *Two important passages where women characters are used in a polemical situation with the respected. One of the passages is from Mark, while the other — probably after a long, independent history*

*in the growing traditions — has found its way into the Fourth
Gospel.*
(a)   The attack on the Pharisees, and the example of the poor widow
(Mark 12, 38-44; Luke 20, 47; 21, 1-4).
(b)   Jesus and the woman caught in adultery (John 7, 53-8, 11).
   3.   *A series of parables found only in the Matthean tradition.*
(a)   The parable of the yeast (Matthew 13, 33).
(b)   The parable of the two sons (Matthew 21, 28-32).
(c)   The parable of the wise and the foolish virgins (Matthew 25,
1-13).
   4.   *The anointing of Jesus in Bethany, a narrative that can be
found, in a variety of forms, in all four Gospel traditions* (Mark 14,
3-9; Matthew 26, 6-13; John 12, 1-8. See Luke 7, 36-50).
   5.   *The presence of women at the cross, the burial and the empty
tomb of Jesus. This is again found, in a variety of forms, through
all four Gospel traditions* (Mark 15, 40-16, 8; Matthew 27, 55-28,
10; Luke 23, 49-24, 11; John 20, 1-2, 11-18).
The sheer quantity of this material is impressive, especially when one
notices that I have omitted all the specifically Lucan material, as I
intend to deal with that within the context of my chapter on Luke's
particular use of women characters in his Gospel. There is, however,
even more material from the Gospels that deserves our attention.
Although female characters may not be actively involved in these
particular narratives, there are some important indications in them
that throw further light upon Jesus' attitude towards woman:[11]
(a)   Looking upon a woman lustfully (Matthew 5, 28).
(b)   The divorce material (Mark 10, 1-12; Matthew 19, 1-12 and 5,
31-32; Luke 16, 18).
(c)   Jesus' true family (Mark 3, 31-35; Matthew 12, 46-50; Luke 8,
19-21).
A full-scale study of all this material would lead us into another large
volume in its own right. I merely intend to comment as concisely as I
can on each text, linking each passage to our theme as I pass through.
The reader will notice that very similar themes emerge time and
again.

1.   THE MIRACLE STORIES

(a)   *The cure of Peter's mother-in-law: Mark 1, 29-31* (see also
Matthew 8, 14-15; Luke 4, 38-39).
As Simon's mother-in-law lies sick with a fever, Jesus goes to her and
touches her. The fever departs, and she *serves* them. There are two
important details to be noticed, if we wish fully to appreciate all the

implications of this passage. First, Jesus touches a woman by taking her by the hand, showing extraordinary internal freedom. Then, as perhaps even today, a respected religious leader would not take any woman by the hand. It is useless to speculate on his prior knowledge of Peter's mother-in-law. That sort of thinking goes beyond anything indicated in the text itself. Next, he allows himself to be served by this woman. That may appear normal enough to us, but no self-respecting Rabbi would allow such a thing. As Rabbi Samuel (died in AD254) has said: 'One must under no circumstances be served by a woman, be she adult or child.'[12] In the Marcan vision of the life of Jesus, the very 'first day' of Jesus' public ministry (see Mark 1, 21-34) is highlighted by this extraordinarily new approach to a woman. In fact, the episode of the curing of Simon's mother-in-law forms the center of the day's activities: he cures the possessed man (1, 21-28), raises the fever-stricken woman (vv. 29-31) and then cures all who come to him (vv. 32-34). Our episode is deliberately placed at the center of a day's miraculous presence of the overpowering reign of God, vanquishing the reign of evil, symbolized by devil possession and physical illness.

(b) *The healing of the woman with a hemorrhage: Mark 5, 24-34* (see also Matthew 9, 20-22; Luke 8, 43-48).
It is important to notice the contrast in this narrative between the 'good sense' of the disciples:

You see the crowd pressing around you, and yet you say, 'Who *touched* me?' (v.31)

and the complete self-abandonment of the woman:

If I *touch* even his garments I shall be made well (v.28).

This impression is further heightened by the description of the woman's awe-filled approach to Jesus, when her ploy to touch Jesus has been unmasked:

The woman, knowing what had been done to her, came in fear and trembling and fell down before him and told him the whole truth (v.33).

The response of Jesus is at the one time in praise of the woman and a correction for the disciples. The language used by Jesus shifts from 'woman' to 'daughter', to express his oneness with her way of faith:

Daughter, your faith has made you well (v.34).

Again we see Jesus' readiness to break through the ways of the 'righteous', so full of common sense and wordly wisdom, to focus his affection and attention elsewhere, to allow contact between a woman who would have been judged by those 'righteous ones' as in a continual state of ritual uncleanness, because of her flow of blood, and himself, a religious leader. For the first time in the Gospel of Mark we find the use of a woman to show the right and the wrong way to come to Jesus in faith.

(c) *The raising of Jairus' daughter: Mark 5, 21-24, 35-43* (see also Matthew 9, 18-19, 23-26; Luke 8, 40-42, 49-56).
The reader will have noticed that this story, in all three Synoptic Gospels, is used as a sort of 'frame' around the account of the cure of the woman with the hemorrhage. If we look closely at how Mark has used his material in gradually developing the argument of his Gospel, we find that we have a deliberate gathering of 'woman stories' to form the conclusion of a section of Mark's Gospel that has been dominated by Jesus' miraculous activity. From Mark 4, 35 onwards there has been a gradual crescendo of increasingly significant miracles:
4, 35-41: A nature miracle, as he calms the storm and the waters: 'even the wind and the sea obey him' (4, 41).
5, 1-20: A spectacular victory over the demons, as he drives out a legion of unclean spirits from the Gerasene demoniac.
5, 21-24: The request from Jairus.
5, 25-35: A victory over human illness, as he cures the woman with the haemorrhage.
5, 35-43: A victory over death itself, in the raising of Jairus' daughter.

Notice the progression from natural disturbances to human illness, to a victory over death itself, and notice also that both of the people involved in the final two miracles are women. There is a further connection between the final two passages, which is never noticed by the commentators: the frankness, honesty and healing *touch* of Jesus. We have already pointed out Jesus' readiness to touch and to be touched by a woman, indicating a marvellous freedom from constraint and prejudices. In Mark 5, 41 we again read: 'Taking her by the hand' (see earlier, 1, 31). There follows a very precise indication of the girl's age, as we are told in 5, 42 that she was twelve years old. Most commentators make nothing of this indication, and would agree with Vincent Taylor that this 'is added to explain the walking'.[13] The reader may have been led to think that she was only an infant without this indication of her age. Yet, given the interest that

Mark seems to show in Jesus' revolutionary 'touching' of women, and given that the precise year of 'twelve' is indicated, could this have been added to increase the shock created by Jesus' action? She was of marriageable age! As R. E. Brown has explained, in reference to Jewish marriage practices:

> The consent, usually entered into when the girl was between twelve and thirteen years old, would constitute a legally ratified marriage in our times, since it gave the young man rights over the girl. She was henceforth his wife.[14]

In such a situation, Jesus' 'taking her by the hand' is again an ambiguous gesture for a religious leader. When this affectionate gesture is further enriched by the beautifully caring Aramaic expression, *Talitha cumi*, 'My dearest little one, stand up',[15] retained in the Greek version of Mark because of its powerful impact and its eloquence, the encounter between Jesus and this young woman takes on a very special significance. Over against this impressive encounter, one must read of the commotion and disbelief of all the people:

> They laughed at him . . . and they were overcome with amazement (vv.40 and 42).

Although we are told of their amazement, there is no indication that this miracle moved even one of them towards Jesus in faith. It appears that we have here a powerful contrast between all those incredulous scoffers surrounding the scene — and the loving gentleness of those at its center: Jesus of Nazareth and a young woman.

(d) *The Syrophoenician woman: Mark 7, 24-30* (see also Matthew 15, 21-28).
We must be careful, in a study of this nature, not to force the reading of the text. Nevertheless, we are now glancing at a section of Mark's Gospel where the question of the Gentile mission is most clearly dealt with (see 7, 24-8, 10). This is made very clear through Mark's geographical indications in 7, 24 and 31:

> He arose and went away though the region of Tyre and Sidon . . . He returned from the region of Tyre, and went through Sidon to the Sea of Galilee, through the region of the Decapolis.

This would be an extraordinarily roundabout way of going from Tyre to the lake, but such a journey would keep Jesus always in Gentile territory. For these reasons, Mark constructs this roundabout journey. Further, there are several references to Gentile themes in the second multiplication of the bread, especially in 8, 3:

If I send them away hungry to their homes they will faint on the way; *and some of them have come a long way.*

and also in the use of the number 'seven' in verses 5 and 8, in contrast to the use of 'twelve' in the first multiplication (see 6, 43). At the head of this whole section stands the vivid story of the faith of the Syrophoenician woman. Mark 7, 1-23 has prepared the way by showing the falsity of traditional, but hypocritical, Jewish ways. The woman, in petitioning for her possessed daughter (another woman!), has no human rights, and she can lay no claim to Jesus' power and authority — and Jesus tells her so (v.27). Her answer shows a deep recognition of her nothingness.

She comes making no legal claims and pleading no special merits, but just as she is, empty-handed and in need, and dares only to accept God's gift in Jesus. Thereby is exemplified the contrast between Jewish legalism and the faith that waits on God.[16]

However, what must be further noticed is that *a woman* is used to indicate this faith, as she asks for the curing of her *daughter.*

Already, from this rapid analysis of four Marcan miracle stories where women play a leading role, we can see some common themes emerging:

(a) There was an extraordinarily deep inner peace and freedom in Jesus of Nazareth, which shows that he was ultimately free from all culturally, historically and even religiously conditioned constraints and prejudices. This has been made particularly clear through Jesus' allowing himself to both touch and be touched by women of all conditions. It is also to be found in his allowing himself to be served by Simon's mother-in-law.

(b) There is the repeated use of a woman and a women's faith in contrast to a lack of faith in the self-righteousness of legalistic Judaism (5, 35-43: Jairus' daughter and 7, 24-30: the Syrophoenician woman) and of his own disciples (5, 24-34: the woman with a hemorrhage).

(c) Woman characters are used in a situation of primacy, at least in Mark's Gospel. The first Gentile to come to faith is the Syrophoenician woman, and the culminating demonstration of the irresistible presence of the active reign of God made present in Jesus is shown in two great miracles that involve women, who are deliberately portrayed as having an intimate personal contact with Jesus: the woman with the hemorrhage, and Jairus' daughter.[17]

2. THE CONFLICT STORIES

(a) *The widow's mite: Mark 12, 38-44* (see also Luke 20, 47; 21, 1-4).
The whole of Mark 12 is dominated by a series of conflicts between Jesus and the Jewish authorities. They challenge him on taxes (vv. 13-17), the resurrection from the dead (vv.18-27) and the first of all commandments (vv.28-34). These conflicts lead Jesus into a direct attack upon the hypocrisy of the Scribes, who have all the correct garb, and all the places of honor, but 'who devour widow's houses and for a pretence make long prayers' (v.40). Here we are at the key issue. Jesus has no desire for pomp and ceremony; he wants his disciples, both women and men, to give their all. The Scribes, the Pharisees and the Sadducees, with whom Jesus has argued up to this point, are only pretending to be 'God-people'. He rounds off his condemnation of such a form of faith and religiosity with the story of the widow's mite. The widow—so despised and, above all, abused by the 'righteous ones' (see v.40)—gives her all:

She has put in everything she had (v.44).

She has lived out in practice the ideals expressed in the vocation of the first disciples, where Jesus has called them to leave all and to 'follow' him (see 1, 16-20; 2, 13-14; 3, 13-19).[18] After our study of the miracle stories, where we found that woman characters were regularly used *over against* the recognized Jewish authorities, and also over against the very lack of faith in Jesus' own disciples, it is interesting to see that this concluding section of Jesus' encounter with Judaism is rounded off with the use of a further woman character to show what it really means to be a disciple. That the whole issue is concerned with true and false discipleship can be seen from verses 43-44:

And he called his *disciples* to him, and said to them . . .
'she . . . has put in everything she had'.

The passage is certainly an attack on the legalism of the Jewish authorities, but it reaches further. Mark tells his story for his own disciples, and for the disciples of all time, as all are capable of thinking that faith and its practice can be 'controlled'. The message of Jesus, correcting such false views, comes to us through the example of a woman who gave her all.

(b) *The woman taken in adultery: John 7, 53-8, 11.*
This beautifully written passage breaks unexpectedly into the section of the Fourth Gospel devoted to the Feast of Tabernacles (John 7, 1-10, 21), and is universally recognized as a foreign insertion that has come into the Johannine text as we now have it. It is absent from all important early manuscripts, and when it does begin to appear, it can be found in a variety of places throughout the Gospels.[19]

We cannot hope to examine all the historical and textual complexities of this passage. It is clearly a synoptic-type passage and — as should be clear from what we have already seen — it may well reflect an experience of the historical Jesus that has been kept alive in the tradition, and which has eventually found its way, fortunately, into John. We must examine the story in its own right, and there are a variety of features that merit our attention.

Once more we must notice that Jesus is presented in a situation of conflict. After setting the scene of Jesus' teaching 'all the people' in the Temple (7, 53-8, 2), John presents the Scribes and the Pharisees. They lead in a woman who had been caught in adultery. They publicly accuse the woman, and then challenge Jesus. They know what Moses would think of such a sinful situation, but:

What do you say about her? (v.5)

There is an obviously contrived use of the woman to pit Jesus against the teachings of Moses. To clarify this, the Evangelist adds his note:

This they said to test him, that they might have some charge to bring against him (v.6).

The polemic is very strong and very public — and the woman is a mere trapping in the conflict! In the 'game' being played by the Scribes and the Pharisees the woman, as such, really has no place except as an excuse to debate the Law. She will suit ideally for them to instrumentalize for their own purposes: to teach Jesus a point or two about the Law of Moses.

Jesus' challenge — that the one without sin cast the first stone (v.7) — causes them to drift away, and at the end of the account only Jesus and the woman remain on the scene. She is now no longer an object, a necessary evil. She is now someone who enters into a relationship with Jesus as she is challenged to be all that she can be. Jesus neither condones nor condemns her sin. No one condemns her (v.11). Thus she can take up the challenge to sin no more, the challenge to look squarely at a new self-understanding, and thus to the possibilities of a new life that the men in the earlier part of the story would never have allowed, nor even dreamt of for her. Jesus is not threatened or shocked by a sinner, but he is challenged by the need to lead that sinner, woman or man, into a newness of life — something that traditional Judaism would not have allowed for this particular woman.

Again, the background to this story is the extraordinary peace and inner security of Jesus. It can be felt as he again shows his preparedness to stand traditional values upside down if they mean that a woman thereby becomes a 'thing' — in this case a necessary evil in a debate over a point of law. The issue is that all be given the chance for life, and in this Jesus succeeds, while the Scribes and the Pharisees disappear into failure.

Maria Boulding's incisive commentary on this incident is well worth recording:

The Pharisees are tense, but he is calm and relaxed throughout; he accepts the woman openly and lovingly, as an adult and as a person. He has a sureness of touch; he can handle the situation and the relationship with her because he has nothing to be afraid of in himself. Not only had he no sin, but he must have completely accepted and integrated his own sexuality. Only a man who has done so, or at least begun to do so, can relate properly to women.[20]

3. THE PARABLES

It is generally recognized that the parables of Jesus put us into close contact with the teaching of Jesus, and there are three very short parables found uniquely in the Matthean tradition where women characters are used.

(a) *The parable of the yeast: Matthew 13, 33.*
This short parable, widely accepted as Jesus' authentic teaching on the Kingdom of God, stresses the initiative of God in that Kingdom — the remarkable, rapid, unexpected and inevitable inbreak of his active reigning presence that can give life and vitality to all that it touches:

The kingdom of heaven is like leaven which a woman took and hid in three measures of flour, till it was all leavened.

The use of a woman here probably reflects the fact that a woman was usually responsible for the baking, but again we find Jesus touching the very heart of his preaching: the inbreak of the active reigning presence of God; and again we find that at the centre of the parable, the human agent in all this, stands a woman.

(b) *The parable of the two sons: Matthew 21, 28-32.*
There is some discussion over the original form of this parable, but it may well go back to Jesus himself, almost in the form in which Matthew has found it in his own traditions.[21] Its contents are well known.

One son refuses to work in the vineyard, but repents and does while another is full of good words, but does nothing (vv.28-30). The parable of the two sons leads Jesus to his point: it is the tax collectors and the harlots who will enter the kingdom of heaven before the chief priests and the elders of the people (v.31. See v.23). Again, as the passage runs further, one of our ever-present themes reappears: it is not the righteous ones in the eyes of the world who are the 'God-people', it is to be those who are receptive to the extraordinary newness of the challenge of Jesus of Nazareth. Already with John the Baptist the harlots had shown the way to the hard-headed and self-righteous religious leaders of Israel. This is the case because the latter were not prepared to *repent*, to turn away from their current way of life, because they supposed that there was absolutely no need for such a radical reassessment of their situation and their style of life. Only the sinner aware of her or his nothingness, yet *receptive* to the life-giving power of God's reign that is offered in Jesus can ever hope to enter the kingdom that he proclaimed and lived. Tax collectors and prostitutes are those selected by Jesus as the sort of people who have such openness and receptivity.

(c) *The parable of the wise and the foolish virgins: Matthew 25, 1-13.*
In this famous parable we are dealing with an original parable of Jesus, calling all to be ready to respond to the invitation offered by God to mankind in the coming of Jesus and his preaching of the kingdom. The Matthean tradition has shifted its sense slightly to make stronger reference to the end time and to the final coming of the Son of Man (see especially vv.5-6 and 13, and Matthew's situating of this parable within the overall context of this teaching on the end time in ch.25).[22] Yet, the challenge issued by Jesus is still clearly present. The parable is directed to disciples of all times to be ready, open and receptive to the appearance of the kingdom of God. Apocalypse 19, 6-7, 9 — again using marriage symbolism — has reinterpreted Jesus' original teaching very well:

The Lord our God the almighty reigns.
Let us rejoice and exult and give him the glory,
for the marriage of the Lamb has come . . .
Blessed are those who are invited to the marriage supper of the Lamb.

This is no *future invitation*. It is a *present reality*.

Returning to the central theme of this book, it is again interesting to see Jesus' easy use of woman characters to make his point. Here, however, the women are used to show *both* possibilities. Some are open, receptive and prepared for the coming of the kingdom, and they are wise, but some are not prepared, and they are judged as foolish. While the use of women is certainly closely linked to the way weddings were celebrated in the time of Jesus, and this would have certainly conditioned his use of them in his parable, their use to show the possibility of success or failure in discipleship will reappear later. It becomes most important in such major texts as John 16, 21-24 and Apocalypse 12, 17 and 21.

4. THE ANOINTING OF JESUS IN BETHANY

This account is found, in a variety of forms, in all four Gospel traditions (Mark 14, 3-9; Matthew 26, 6-13; John 12, 1-8. See also Luke 7, 36-50). The Matthean version (Matthew 26, 6-13) is clearly a rewriting of Mark 14, 3-9, but both Luke (7, 36-50) and John (12, 1-8) appear to have a similar story, which may have come to them via their own independent traditions.[24] There is, therefore, every possibility that we are dealing with an event that happened in Jesus' last days, and that has been passed through a variety of traditions. Such a variety of reports of the same basic story is always a good guide to the historicity of the event. It is quite clear, nevertheless, that Mark and Matthew have rewritten the story as a preparation for the death and burial of Jesus in a way that suited their purposes, given the lack of anointing in the urgent burial scenes in both Gospels. Through the anointing at Bethany they show that the manner of Jesus' burial was already foreseen, and that the body of Jesus had already received its due reverence, despite the violent death and rushed burial. In Luke the theme of forgiveness is uppermost (as we shall see when we consider the Lucan material dealing with women), while in John the theme of the preparation of the body for the burial returns, although from a slightly different perspective, given the fact that in the Fourth Gospel Jesus is buried with a regal anointing (see John 19, 38-42).[25] Thus each Evangelist has used an event taken from the living traditions about Jesus, and has told it in his own way, to make his own particular point clear.

Through all of this, however, is it possible to rediscover what the event tells us about Jesus and his attitudes and relationships with women? Through all the retelling of the story, a series of features comes through very clearly.

(a) The event takes place in the presence of either Pharisees (Mark, Matthew and Luke) or disciples (John). Probably both groups were present: the Jewish and the future Christian religious leaders form the public for the scene.

(b) The gesture is marked by a superabundance of both the quality and the quantity of the oils used. This is clearly an indication of affection, trust and abandon to the person of Jesus.

(c) Jesus has again allowed himself to be touched quite intimately by a woman. In Mark and Matthew it is his head which is anointed, while in both Luke and John the feet are anointed. Luke goes even further into the intimacy of the woman's tears washing his feet, her hair used to towel him, and her gentle kissing of Jesus. It is against this background of the intimacy of touch that the Lucan motif of the sinner has been developed. The remarkable freedom of Jesus is again found, this time in a quite spectacular fashion.

(d) The whole event creates difficulty for the 'righteous ones', be they Pharisees (Synoptic Gospels) or disciples (John). Whether it was because of Jesus' intimacy with a woman (Luke) or the problem of the excessive waste of precious ointment (Matthew, Mark and John) need not concern us. They regarded both Jesus and the woman as in the wrong.

(e) Turning their values upside down, Jesus insists upon her 'beautiful deed' (Mark and Matthew) and upon her love (Luke). Ultimately, what matters above all is the recognition of Jesus and an all-encompassing love for him. She demonstrates both of these, and for that reason:

Wherever the Gospel is preached in the whole world,
what she has done will be told in memory of her (Mark 14, 9).

Again we find consistent themes emerging:
(a) The superlative quality of the faith of a woman, over against the well-measured reactions of Jewish leaders and disciples.

(b) Jesus' extraordinary internal freedom and the complete absence of ambiguity in the intimacy of touch is again powerfully present throughout the whole of this encounter.

(c) The woman is clearly presented as a model, a person whose faith in Jesus and whose deeply felt affection for him is presented as a challenge to disciples of all times as 'what she has done will be told in memory of her' (Mark 14, 9).

5. THE WOMEN AT THE TOMB OF JESUS

One of the most outstanding features of the Gospels' treatment of women characters is the universal presence of women at the empty tomb, and their being the first to proclaim the resurrection. It is found in all four Gospels (Mark 15, 40-16, 8; Matthew 27, 55-28, 10; Luke 23, 49-24, 11; John 20, 1-2, 11-18). Once again I must necessarily leave aside the many discussions, both historical and theological, that surround the contemporary scholarly assessment of these texts. I wish simply to reach back and touch what stands behind these four different versions of these crucial events as they are reported by all four Evangelists.[26] I am again presupposing that the Marcan version is the ultimate source for both Matthew and Luke.[27]

Upon those presuppositions, one can list the following events as reasonably common to all accounts:

(a) Women remain close to the Cross of Jesus, despite the absence of the disciples. This is found in all three Synoptic Gospels. John has transformed this into a highly symbolic scene of the Mother-Son relationship between the Mother of Jesus and the Beloved Disciple (John 19, 25-27). They know where he was buried (all Synoptics make this point).

(b) On the morning of the third day, some women, or maybe only one woman (most probably Mary Magdalene) came to visit the tomb. The whole question of whether or not they came to anoint is somewhat confused, and is probably secondary.

(c) The women (woman) find the tomb empty, and they receive there some sort of revelation, explaining that Jesus has been raised, and that they are to announce this to the disciples.

(d) Although Mark closes his Gospel by leaving the women in silence, the women (woman) almost certainly did proclaim something like Luke 24, 34: 'the Lord has been raised' (see also 1 Corinthians 15, 4). This stands behind the accounts of Matthew and Luke, as they rewrote Mark's version in the light of their own traditions, and John's use of his Mary Magdalene tradition.

(e) The proclamation of the women is not believed by the disciples. The Gospels, including Mark (especially Mark!) are remarkable in their consistent presentation of the doubt and unfaith of the disciples, both at the proclamation of the resurrection and at the appearances (see Mark 16, 8; Matthew 28, 16-17; Luke 24, 10-12, 13-35; John 20, 2-10).

What I have just listed as a 'minimum' that can be distilled from our various accounts would be widely accepted. The interpretation of this 'minimum' could be another matter! Nevertheless, continuing my own argument, it appears to me that our common themes emerge once again.

(a) It is women whose faith and loyalty to Jesus sees them through the trauma of his death and burial, and eventually leads them to proclaim: 'The Lord has been raised'. There is a *primacy* in both the quality of the women's faith, and in their being the first to come to faith in the risen Lord.

(b) This takes place within the context of a group of disciples who have fled in fear (see especially Mark 14, 50, and the parabolic comment upon their flight in vv.51-52: the young man who 'followed' but, when threatened, ran away *naked in his nothingness*). The same disciples are universally presented as refusing to accept the Easter proclamation of the women. The faith of women stands out in strong contrast to the lack of faith among the male disciples, including the 'pillars' of the discipleship group.

The consistency of this theme across the whole Gospel tradition is a good indication of a strong recollection in the early Church that women were the first to witness the empty tomb, and that they were the primary witnesses to the resurrection. The fact that the experience of the women is not found in what is probably the earliest *written* account of the Easter events — the confession of faith in 1 Corinthians 15, 1-7 — does not destroy the evidence of the Gospels. We are dealing with two different forms of literature. Paul is not writing a Gospel, but he is making use of a confession of faith that has come to him from the pre-Pauline Churches for his particular purposes.[28] One of those purposes (the most important for the Corinthian situation?) was to include himself, 'one untimely born' (v.8), among 'the apostles', a uniquely masculine group. It also appears to me that the reference to 'on the third day' in 15, 4 does take us back to the experience of the women at the tomb, as that expression had its birth into the language of the early Church when, in fact, women found a tomb empty 'on the third day'.[29]

There are good reasons to argue that somewhere behind all of this important material from the Gospel traditions that we have just glanced at there stands an authentic memory from the life of Jesus, no matter how much they may have been remodelled by the Evangelists, or the traditions before them.[30] This evidence generally leads scholars to conclude that Jesus' physical contact with women, his openess with them, his preparedness to share life with them — even those considered least important and least worthy of consideration by the culture and religious practice of his contemporaries — was something quite revolutionary. It is always possible, of course, that the use of women in Mark's Gospel is a sophisticated technique invented by that Evangelist, and simply repeated by the others who used him as a source. It could be claimed that he used women as a foil to show the weakness of the supposedly strong, be they Jewish religious leaders (see Mark 12, 41-43) or disciples of Jesus (see Mark 5, 24-34 and 14, 3-9). This appears unlikely to me. Given the insignificant role of woman in first-century Jewish society, Mark has taken over something quite unique from the life of Jesus, even though, as we have seen, he has certainly used the material in his own way, to make his own particular theological point clear.

It should be further pointed out that the theme of a reversal of values, exemplified by this continual use of women to show the strength of the weak and the weakness of the supposedly strong, is not a Marcan invention. However important it may be to his theology, it is something that Mark and his community received from Jesus of Nazareth, and that Jesus himself received from his deep involvement in God's plan as demonstrated throughout the sacred history of his people.[31] From these passages that have women protagonists, it appears that one could confidently say that Jesus of Nazareth opened a new era in the history of women. The later preaching of the Christian Church will go its various ways in the interpretation and application of the place and function of women within a Christian community, sometimes positively and sometimes negatively, as I hope to show as I proceed. However, whichever way it went, it is of vital importance to appreciate the fact that the later Church did not initiate the specifically Christian attitude to woman. It had its beginnings in the person, teaching and attitudes of Jesus of Nazareth.

This can be further seen in a series of passages from the Gospels where women do not actually appear, but where Jesus' teaching shows that he has initiated a whole new way of speaking about women. Within the context of Jewish law and practice, all sins in the area of adultery were sins against man.[32] A man who had sexual relations with another man's wife committed adultery, but it was not adultery for a non-married woman to have sexual relations with a married man. Prostitution was sinful but tolerated. Indeed it may have been necessary for survival for some women, and it was as necessary a 'trade' to satisfy the egoism of the male then as it is now. Judah was not regarded as guilty for taking Tamar, whom he thought was a prostitute. On the contrary, it was the already pregnant Tamar who was almost stoned to death (Genesis 38, 12-26). David was seen and judged as sinning against Uriah when he took Bathsheba. The woman and her experience are not even mentioned in the account of those events in 2 Samuel 11-12. When Nathan castigates David he says:

Why have you despised the word of the Lord, to do what is evil in his sight? You have smitten Uriah the Hittite with the sword, and have taken his wife to be your wife, and have slain him with the sword of the Ammonites (2 Samuel 12, 9).

What Bathsheba made of all of this we can only guess!

Although prostitution was regarded as a sin, it was not penalized (see Leviticus 19, 29; 21, 7; Deuteronomy 23, 17). Of course, the sinfulness was only on the part of the woman. A man who visited a prostitute was not regarded in the same way as the woman who gave herself to prostitution. The same male-oriented legislation stands behind the law on rape. Rape was primarily a crime against the father whose daughter was raped (see Exodus 22, 16-17; Deuteronomy 22, 28-29), just as adultery was a crime against the husband of the woman involved (see, on all this, the indications of Deuteronomy 22, 13-30 and Proverbs 6, 26-35).

Into this situation Jesus speaks boldly:

You have heard that it was said, 'You shall not commit adultery'. But I say to you that every one who looks at a woman lustfully has already committed adultery with her in his heart (Matthew 5, 27-28).

The woman is no longer a 'thing' that somehow is caught up in a whole series of male-oriented attitudes. She is a person to whom all respect, love and honor is due. No more male leering and joking about possible pleasures; they are to be replaced with relationships of mutual love and respect, where a man and a woman can be one — at all levels.

The discussions over divorce were also male-oriented.[33] In the time of Jesus the divorce laws were discussed on the basis of Deuteronomy 24, 1:

When a man takes a wife and marries her, if then she finds no favour in his eyes because he has found *some indecency* in her, and he writes her a bill of divorce and puts it in her hand and sends her out of his house and she departs out of his house . . .

There were two schools of thought. A Rabbi Shammai took a hard line, and insisted that the all-important expression 'some indecency' had to refer to some serious moral defect *on the part of the woman.* In that case, the bill of divorce could be written. Another case was argued by Rabbi Hillel. He claimed that any cause at all would fulfil the requirements of 'some indecency'. The two examples cited in Jewish documents that report Hillel's position are: if there is a more attractive woman available, or if the cooking is burnt! Notice, yet again, that the giving of the bill of divorce depends entirely upon defects *on the part of the woman.*

Once one is aware of this debate, which was going on in the time of Jesus, the question of the Pharisees in the following discussion leads Jesus to speak boldly against such a situation:

And Pharisees came up and in order to test him asked, 'Is it lawful for a man to divorce his wife?' . . . But Jesus said to them . . . 'From the beginning of creation 'God made them male and female.' 'For this reason a man shall leave his father and mother and be joined to his wife, and the two shall become one.' . . . What therefore God has joined together, let no man put assunder (Mark 10, 2, 6-9).

This revolutionary teaching of Jesus is as extraordinary today as it was then. Here we have an explicit contrast drawn between the ways of men, society, custom and culture: the bill of divorce; and God's ways from the beginning: a quality of mutuality and love that is so intense that man and woman become one. The whole sexual situation *must not* be the imposition of the will and the body of man upon the will and the body of woman. God did not create man and woman to live in such a situation. Any legislation of divorce that makes woman the 'tennis ball' that can be struck from partner to partner must be wrong — yet such was the case in the world of Jesus. This could not be, and again we see the extraordinary freedom of Jesus as he takes on the Law of Moses itself to assert that 'the two shall become one' and that no man must dare to interfere between this oneness created by mutual respect and love. Such a oneness is God-given: what right has man to interfere?[34]

As we close these reflections upon Jesus of Nazareth, a nagging question must be solved. What is it in Jesus that creates such a revolutionary newness? The answer has to be found in his own conviction that in his presence there was the inauguration of a new world where God is allowed to be God, and where men and women — children of the same God, his Father — were allowed to be men and women — brothers and sisters equally.

Jesus of Nazareth came to establish a new reign of God where all accepted fears, taboos, distinctions and divisions between male and female have been wiped away:

'Who are my mother and my brothers?' And looking around on those who sat about him, he said, 'Here are my mother and brothers! Whoever does the will of God is my brother, and sister and mother' (Mark 3, 33-34. See also Matthew 12, 46-50; Luke 8, 19-21).

What a different place the world would be if such were the case! What a different person I would be if I were able to respond joyfully and unceasingly to the challenge of Jesus' love, respect, freedom and care with the women in his life. Perhaps nowhere in the history of mankind has any man been to woman what Jesus was to woman — but the challenge of Jesus stands before us all:

(Woman) had never known a man like this Man — there never has been such another. A prophet and teacher who never nagged at them, never flattered or coaxed or patronized; who never made arch jokes about them . . . who rebuked without querulousness and praised without condescension . . . who never mapped out their sphere for them, never urged them to be feminine or jeered at them for being female; who had no axe to grind and no uneasy male dignity to defend; who took them as he found them and was completely unself-conscious. There is no act, no sermon, no parable in the whole Gospel that borrows its pungency from female perversity; nobody could possibly guess from the words and deeds of Jesus that there was anything 'funny' about woman's nature.[35]

PAUL:
A TRADITION DEVELOPS [36]

A superficial reading of Paul's letters in translation indicates that the Apostle of the Gentiles has little to help us in our attempt to trace a positive New Testament picture of woman. There are several passages, especially 1 Corinthians 11, 2-16, where the so-called question of the head-covering is discussed, and 1 Corinthians 14, 33b-35, where women are told to be submissive to their husbands, that have long stood at the heart of a male superiority complex that has dogged the Church since her earliest days. I have already mentioned that the post-Easter preaching and writing of the early Church went in different directions, as it interpreted and put into practice the teaching of Jesus on woman. It could appear that Paul swerved radically away from what we have discovered was the attitude and teaching of Jesus. In recent years there have been attempts to rehabilitate Paul by short-circuiting these difficult passages through a claim that they are both non-Pauline interpolations.[37] The suggestion is that the authentic Pauline teaching had to be softened down by his followers, so when the letters eventually came to be copied and passed from generation to generation, these passages were inserted by Paul's successors, in order to accommodate his teaching to the social and cultural situation of the Church's involvement in the first-century world. It appears that there are good reasons, both theological and textual, for rejecting the authenticity of 1 Corinthians 14, 33b-35,[38] but a recent discussion headed by Jerome Murphy-O'Connor shows that the passage in 1 Corinthians 11 both belongs to Paul and reflects an underlying positive theology of women; but we must discuss this at a larger stage.[39]

Unfortunately, many discussions of Paul's attitude to women are dominated by those few rather negative passages that I have just mentioned. This means that other, more centrally important, passages are often missed. What must be seen as decisive in any discussion of the Pauline material is his overarching theology of the Christian life as being a 'life in Christ'.[40]

At the center of Paul's Gospel stands the story of a Jesus crucified but risen. To everyone who is prepared to lose himself in love and service unto death, this Jesus offers a newness of life that can be ours *now* (see for example, Romans 5, 1-5; Galatians 4, 4-7) as we participate — even on this side of death — in what Paul continually calls 'life in Christ'. The concept of the Christian life being a 'life in Christ' is something that dominates Paul's thought. From a reading of Romans alone, one can find that almost every aspect of the Christian life is somewhere described as 'in Christ'. The Christian is baptized 'in Christ' (Romans 6, 3), lives his every day life, greets people, has his glory and the life of the Spirit — 'in Christ' (see Romans 6, 11; 8, 2; 9, 1; 15, 17; 16, 3-10), forms one body with other Christians 'in Christ' (Romans 12, 5) and finally has redemption and eternal life 'in Christ' (Romans 6, 11).

There is a lot of scholarly discussion over the meaning of the Pauline expression 'in Christ'. This is understandable, as all scholars agree that it communicates, for Paul, what he understands to be the very heart of Christian living. For Paul, to exist as a Christian, to *be* a Christian in an active, committed way, meant to live 'in Christ'. Sometimes scholars become too single-minded. Simply to study Paul's use of the expression 'in Christ' is insufficient. It is sounder to range a little more widely, and to look at some texts where he uses this central expression with some other famous images. Often Paul speaks of the Christian's 'putting on Christ', and his 'becoming the new man'. Unfortunately, these two expressions are often taken as indicating some sort of mystical experience, or the moral improvement that must accompany baptism into Christianity. There is much more to it. There are two famous Pauline texts where the images of 'in Christ', 'putting on Christ' and 'becoming the new man' are all used in close association with one another:

As many of you as were baptized *into Christ* have *put on Christ*. There is neither Jew nor Greek, there is neither slave nor free, neither male nor female; for *you are all one in Christ, Jesus* (Galatians 3, 27-28).

You have *put on the new man . . . where* there cannot be Greek and Jew, uncircumcised and circumcised, barbarian, Scythian, slave, freeman, *but Christ is all in all* (Colossians 3, 10 A.T.).

There are some important facts which must be seen and understood for a proper appreciation of these texts. First, they come from two quite different periods of Paul's life, and thus were written within the context of two quite different experiences. The Letter to the Galatians was probably written in AD 55, while Paul was in the full flood of his missionary activity.

Colossians, commonly called a 'prison letter', appears to have been written towards the end of his life, presumably some time in the early 60s. It is commonly recognized that between the younger and the later Paul there is sometimes a maturation and even an alteration in his thought. For example, his thinking on the subject of the end time shifted quite seriously between the beginning of his career, evidenced in 1 Thessalonians, and his last letters, the so-called 'prison letters' (especially Colossians and Ephesians). This and similar developments can be easily traced by comparing the different way in which he treats the same themes across his lengthy letter-writing career. As well as the difference in Paul's personal experience and situation, Galatians and Colossians were directed at two quite different communities, or groups of Churches, which had very different theological and pastoral problems. The Galatian community was running the serious risk of turning back to the protection of the Law and thus, according to Paul, they were risking a loss of the unique freedom that had been won for them through the death and resurrection of Jesus Christ (see Galatians 5, 1). The Colossians seemed to be facing problems from a more speculative, libertine, syncretistic stream of Jewish thought (see, for example, Colossians 2, 8, 16, 18, 21-23). Yet, despite these very important *differences* in place, time and argument, the texts we are examining are clearly *very similar*. This is quite striking.

There can be no doubt, in the light of the above observations, that the argument treated in these two texts is absolutely central to Pauline thought, and it will not allow any alteration or adaptation with the change of time and circumstances. Both texts share the lists of traditionally hostile groups: Greek and Jew, circumcised and uncircumcised, slave and freeman, *male and female*. It is important, in order to fully understand Paul's argument, to recall that in the first century *these divisions were an accepted matter of fact*. No one in his right mind would have suggested that people should *not* have been divided according to those lists—but Paul did! Both of our passages, reflecting a central idea in Pauline thought (see also Romans 10, 12-13; 1 Corinthians 12, 12-13; Ephesians 2, 11-22), claim that these accepted divisions are finished in an entirely new situation into which the Christian has entered.

It is important to notice my indication that Paul was speaking into a 'new situation'. It appears that he saw 'life in Christ' as some sort of change of situation that carries with it a spatial concept. The new situation involved in 'life in Christ' for the members of the Pauline communities was not just a new frame of mind or a new set of attitudes. Paul seems to claim that by becoming a Christian, the ex-Pagan or Jew has moved into a 'new place', *where* things are different. In the passage from Galatians, Paul describes this new situation as a place where all constitute 'one man', while in Colossians he goes even further with his spatial idea, and explicitly states that 'the new man' is a place *where* (Greek: *hopou*) the divisions so commonly accepted can no longer exist.

This may appear to be a difficult concept, but a little reflection on the situation of the earliest Christians should help to clarify things. It is not only Paul who has this idea. A sense of 'motion' from one place to another is also found in a famous Johannine expression, which almost defies translation. For John, true faith is 'faith into', or 'faith unto' (Greek: *pisteuein eis*) Jesus Christ. This may be difficult in English, but it reflected the concrete experience of the earliest Christians. In fact, to become Christians they did, in practice, make a journey from one place to another, from one situation to another. They literally 'crossed the road' from synagogue or temple *into* the Christian community. In one of the earliest passages we have from Paul he describes the process well:

You turned to God from idols, to serve a living and true God, and wait for his Son from heaven, whom he raised from the dead, Jesus who delivers us from the wrath to come (1 Thessalonians 1, 9).

Once we see and understand just what happened in the real-life experience of these first Christians, then the Pauline and the Johannine expressions indicating that conversion into Christianity led the convert into a new sphere of existence can be more easily understood. The language they used reflected a lived experience.

I hope that this fairly detailed analysis has made it clear that 'life in Christ' is not a new set of moral habits nor some sort of mystical experience. It is deeply rooted in the real-life experience of the Pauline Christians. It refers to their *new sphere of existence*. To become a Christian, in the Pauline vision of things, meant to go away from one *place*, firmly controlled by custom and culture imposed upon it by temple and synagogue practice, into another *place*, where all the normally accepted barriers between men and women, imposed by custom and culture, were brushed away. What Judaism and Paganism saw as normal was regarded as impossible in the new situation of Christianity. Because of baptism, the insertion of the Christian into the death and resurrection of Jesus Christ (see Romans 6, 3-4), there existed an entirely new situation where others formed an *integral* part. To spell this out more clearly: the Pauline notion of 'life in Christ', Paul's central understanding of what it meant to be Christian, is nothing less than an insistence that our very existence as Christians is not something that we personally possess; it is a radically new situation of life and love into which we enter through baptism into the Church. To be a Christian, therefore, means to participate in the lives of others, to share, to break down barriers that

39

divide us. It would have been impossible for Paul to imagine an *autonomous* Christian. For Paul, autonomy and Christianity would have been terms that contradicted each other. We exist and have our lives *as Christians* only in the profound openness to the sharing of life and love with other Christians. It is within this sphere of the sharing of life, where all divisions are eliminated, that we can justifiably claim to be living as Christians.

A little reflection upon our own situations will show that it must be this way. Not one of us became a Christian, entered into the wonderful mystery of the Church and the life of Grace, under our own steam! This was given to us by people who, in their own turn, drawn by the gift of God's love, were prepared to share what they already enjoyed: our parents or the people who drew us by the quality of their own Christian lives into this shared life 'in Christ'. Once we are 'in Christ', to use Pauline language, to abandon this sharing of life is to go 'out' of the life that has the imitation of Christ's loving gift of self as its lifeblood. This means that one abandons an authentic Christianity, even if we happen to have our *private* Mass and communion, and live according to a literal observance of the commandments all our lives. I am not saying that such a person is not saved. That is another question. I am saying, however, that he or she is no longer Christian, living in the heart of the love and freedom that is the result of a 'life in Christ'.

For freedom Christ has set us free; stand fast, therefore, and do not submit again to the yoke of slavery (Galatians 5, 1).

This profound vision touches all aspects of the Christian life. No genuine Christian can live for himself, because his very existence *as a Christian* would be thus lost to him. We have our Christian lives only in so far as we depend upon other Christians, only in so far as we continually give to other Christians and receive from other Christians. We are Christians, we exist as Christians in, through, for and because of other Christians — as we are all caught up in the Grace-filled mystery of our 'life in Christ'. While the rest of the New Testament does not systematically work through a theology of 'life in Christ' as Paul does, the various authors simply presuppose such a life as their first premise. There is an extraordinary agreement in all the New Testament literature that there is only one law in Christianity: the new law of love. It has to be so, as to love and to allow yourself to be loved is the only way in which human beings can hope to experience the reality that Paul calls 'life in Christ': to be, to exist for the other. This is the only way to authentic Christian life: a mutual reciprocity and interdependence that knows no barriers.

There are many pastoral and theological consequences that flow from this Pauline vision of the essence of Christianity,[41] but as far as this reflection is concerned, we must see that at the *heart* of the Pauline vision stands a shattering insistence, in the light of first-century ideas about women, that in the new world of Christian faith there could no longer be a distinction of quality, or a division of any nature, between men and women. 'In Christ' all culturally and historically conditioned prejudices have been broken down. It is from this premise that one must interpret the more difficult passages in Paul, and not vice versa. There can be little doubt that Paul would have had great difficulties fighting against firmly entrenched cultural and religious prejudices, to put his theology into practice. The interpolation in 1 Corinthians 14, 33b-35, along with the subordinate position given to women in the Church in the Pastoral Epistles (see, for example, 1 Timothy 2, 11-12; 3, 9-11 and Titus 2, 4-6; 5, 5), show that he was not always successful.[42] What has happened over the centuries — indeed already by the first half of the second century — is an 'accommodating' of the radical Pauline message to again set up barriers between male and female. Of course, the later Church made no distinction between the authentically Pauline letter, the later interpolations to these letters, and the Pastoral Epistles, written well after Paul, adapting the Pauline message to a later time and to the changed situation of the Church — yet still written under the pseudonym of 'Paul' (see 1 Timothy 1, 1; 2 Timothy 1, 1; Titus 1, 1).[43] In this way Paul has come to be known as a misogynist and a 'woman-hater' on false evidence. At the heart of the Pauline Gospel stands an authentic interpretation of the attitudes and the teaching of Jesus of Nazareth: in Christ the age-old barriers between male and female have been brushed aside.

Thus, I would insist, Paul's radical breakthrough was a challenge to the early Church, and 1 Corinthians 11, 2-16 must be interpreted in that light. Jerome Murphy-O'Connor has done this in a striking new suggestion. He has argued that in this passage:

Paul is, in fact, using *two* lines of argument. The first is a differentiation of sexes based on Genesis 1, 26-27 and 2, 18-22 (vv.7-9). The second is that the recreated woman has an authority equal to that of man (vv.10-12). The two are related . . . inasmuch as the woman has this power precisely as a woman. New status is accorded to woman, not as an ambiguous being whose 'unfeminine' hair-do was an affront to generally accepted conventions. Hence, in so far as her way of doing her hair clearly defines her sex, it becomes a symbol of the authority she enjoys.

The infamous problem of the wearing of the veil (a mistranslation, as head-covering is mentioned, and that may refer to many forms of covering the head — not necessarily to a veil) is not to place woman in a subordinate role, but to insist that the woman who leads the assembly in prayer and prophecy must *appear as a woman*. This (in the Corinthian situation) called for the cessation of 'manly' haircuts, and the return to the 'feminine' covering over their long hair. Murphy-O'Connor translates the troublesome verse 10 as follows: 'She must appear as a woman by the way she dresses her hair'.[44] We must not use this text to discuss whether or not women should wear hats in Church, or whether or not Religious women should wear veils. That is to absolutize the wrong issue, and to miss Paul's point completely. What must be seen as central to his argument is that women in the Church be women, and be seen as women by the way they are dressed, and not as imitations of men!

The key to a correct understanding of the Christian woman is to start with his central belief, indicated by his insistent and clear teaching on the breaking down of all traditional barriers between male and female in the new situation, which he describes as 'in Christ'. One must interpret the difficult and apparently contrasting passages from Paul in the light of his central arguments, and not vice-versa. From there, Paul and the post-Pauline Churches in pastoral difficulties can be easily understood. This phenomenon is not only found in the Pauline corpus. We also see the Johannine letters, written after the Gospel, returning to more 'fixed positions' when faced with the pastoral and theological difficulties that arose in the Church in the post-Gospel period.[45] This thesis needs more teasing out, but the general lines of the argument should be clear. What I would like to claim at this stage is that Paul, the earliest interpreter of the significance and message of Jesus, has *correctly* understood the attitude of Jesus towards women, and has begun to work out his own theological synthesis in perfect accord with that attitude. Thus, we can rightly look to the heart of the Pauline corpus and argue that in Paul there is an inspired understanding of both the behavior and the teaching of Jesus of Nazareth as regards women. As we have already seen, the Pauline letters themselves show that culture and custom were not happy with such an understanding, and every attempt was made to 'tame' Paul and his teaching. Despite this, one can see quite clearly that from Jesus to Paul a new and remarkable Christian tradition as regards woman has been born and has been further developed.[46]

THE GOSPEL OF MATTHEW

It is generally held that Matthew's theological portrait of Jesus leaves little space for any further developments in the early Church's understanding of the role and function of woman. He does take up the Marcan stories, but most scholars would argue that only touches of slight importance are added to them.[47] It appears to me, however, that there are two important Matthean contributions to our discussion. The first is his use of women in Jesus' genealogy (Matthew 1, 1-17),[48] and the second is his rewriting and editing of Mark 3, 31-35 in Matthew 12, 46-50. Apart from these two instances where Matthew places particular stress upon women, he simply retells the Marcan passages. However, given the two instances that we will examine in a little more detail below, his use of Mark's woman passages are not included simply because they were in his source: they are there because he agrees with what was said in his source!

MATTHEW 1, 1-17: THE GENEALOGY OF JESUS

The overall theme of the genealogy of Jesus is made clear in 1, 17:

So all the generations from Abraham to Moses were fourteen generations, and from David to the deportation to Babylon fourteen generations, and from the deportation to Babylon to Christ fourteen generations.

Matthew has used fourteen names, which run from Abraham to David in 1 Chronicles 1-2, and has then repeated that same number three times (the perfection of 'three'). In this way the perfection of all the messianic expectations was fulfilled:

Jesus was born, who is called Christ (1, 16).

Matthew has used this obvious literary scheme to announce that the coming of Jesus of Nazareth, the Messiah, was the end-product of God's careful direction of history. He may have manipulated the *facts* a little, and even invented a name or two, but he has done so to communicate his belief that history from Abraham to Jesus Christ was God's doing.

Given this logical and highly organized scheme of history, one of the puzzles that has been a great source of speculation over the centuries is the regular mentioning of women in this genealogy: Tamar (v.3), Rahab (v.5), Ruth (v.5) and Bathsheba, mentioned as the wife of Uriah the Hittite (v.6). It is most unusual in any ancient near-eastern genealogy, and equally so in the Old Testament genealogies, to give any prominence to women, and scholars have concluded from this that the women are there because Matthew wanted to make a point through his use of their names. A careful reading, even in the English translation, will show that the presence of these women's names breaks into the regular rhythm and structure of a genealogy. Normally there is the rhythmic pattern of

A was the father of B,
B was the father of C,
C was the father of D,

and so on. This pattern is found in almost every verse of Matthew 1, 1-17. The exceptions are immediately obvious, as the name of a woman crops up most unexpectedly:

Judah the father of Perez
and Zerah *by Tamar*, and Perez the father of Hezron,
and Hezron the father of Ram (v.3).

The normal literary pattern of a genealogy has been broken. Why were these women introduced? It has always been recognized that there must have been some single purpose for Matthew's strange introduction of the women. Quite correctly, over the centuries different scholars have sought to discover this purpose by asking what all four of these women had in common, as there must have been some common feature that led Matthew to include them. There have been two classical answers.

(a) *St Jerome*

As far back as the fourth century, Jerome (342-420) sought out this common feature, and he came up with the suggestion that all four of them were sinners, and that Matthew included them to foreshadow the role of Jesus as the Saviour of sinful men and women (see especially the further use of this theme in 1, 21). This suggestion runs into a serious difficulty, however, in the fact that the women were *not* considered to be sinners. Ruth did not sin with Boaz, according to Levirate Law, which demands that the next of kin must marry the widow of his relative, if the male member of the family has died without raising up a son to continue the family name and tradition (Deuteronomy 25, 5-10. See this in practice in Ruth 3, 6-9, 14). While the other three women could be seen as being in some way caught up in unchastity, they do not appear to have been judged as sinners. Tamar was a seductress (Genesis 38), but she was highly regarded in first-century Judaism because she was a woman of determination and adroitness. In fact, already in Genesis 38, 26, Judah (whom she seduced when he forbade her his son, for reasons of superstition) admits that she was in the right, and that he was wrong not to give her to his son. What is even more important is that through her, because of her determination, Judah's line was continued, and thus Israel could eventually come into history.[49]

Rahab is called a prostitute (Joshua 2, 1-21; 6, 17-25), but there is no scene describing any unchaste activity on her part. What is at the center of her story is her being the heroine of the victory of Israel at Jericho, another major turning point in the history of God's people, as they come to take possession of the land. She is responsible for the safety and protection of the Hebrew spies, and is rewarded for her part in the victory at Jericho, as the scarlet cord from her window sees to it that none of her family perish in the slaughter (Joshua 6, 17-25). In early Christian writing she is explicitly hailed as a model of faith (Hebrews 11, 31; The Letter of Clement 21, 1) and the scarlet cord is later paralleled with the flow of blood from the side of Christ, which saved mankind, just as the cord saved her family.

Even Bathsheba's adultery is presented in 2 Samuel 11-12 as David's sin, not hers. Never, in the account of the events themselves, nor in the later reflection of Israel, does she appear as a sinner. This is important, as later reflection upon David tended to 'canonize' him, and faults were quickly laid at other people's doors. The sin with Bathsheba could have easily been explained away through a blackening of Bathsheba's character. This never happens. Later Judaism certainly never saw the sin as of any consequence, as she too played an all-important role in the unfolding of God's plan for Israel. She eventually became the mother of Solomon, and the messianic Davidic line was assured.

Thus Jerome's theory, in the light of how these women were considered by both Jewish and early Christian tradition, fails to convince contemporary scholarship.

(b) *Martin Luther*

Some eleven centuries later, Martin Luther (1483-1546) also saw the importance of this question. He argued that all the women were to be regarded as foreigners, and Matthew includes them in Jesus' genealogy to show that he was related by ancestry to the Gentiles. Rahab and Tamar were Canaanites, and Ruth was a Moabitess. We are not told of the origins of Bathsheba, but since she was married to Uriah the Hittite, there is every possibility that she too was a foreigner. This suggestion would provide a possible solution to the problem, and it would fit in very well with Matthew's theological argument in his infancy narrative. In 1, 1 he announced that Jesus was both Son of David and Son of Abraham. The former places Jesus within Jewish messianic expectations, but his being 'Son of Abraham' looks back to Abraham's vocation to be the father of many nations (see especially Genesis 12, 1-5). The theme of Jesus' place among the Gentiles is again taken up in the story of the Magi in 2, 1-12. However, despite the general suitability of Luther's suggestion, one glaring difficulty remains: the concentration upon the origins of the four women mentioned in verses 3, 5 and 6 has failed to notice that another women is mentioned in verse 16, still well within the genealogy. There are five women mentioned in Matthew 1, 1-17, and any attempt to explain the presence of the women must also include

Mary, of whom Jesus was born, who is called the Christ.

She was a Jewish girl, and thus the suggestion that the women are all foreigners is not universally true. The inclusion of Mary in the discussion has led many contemporary scholars to what I would regard as the correct solution to the problem under discussion.

Now that we have introduced a further woman, can we still find some feature that *all five* of the women share? It appears to me that there are two important common elements that link all five women. (i) In every case there is something extraordinary or irregular in their sexual situation, their union with their partners, or the pregnancy that follows. It was a scandal to those who were 'outside' the mystery of God's plan working through them. That this was also the case with Mary can be seen from Matthew 1, 18-19:

Now the birth of Jesus Christ took place in this way. When his mother Mary had been betrothed to Joseph, before they came together she was found to be with child of the Holy Spirit; and her husband Joseph, being a just man and unwilling to put her to shame, resolved to send her away quietly.

(ii) Despite the irregularities, all of these women, including Mary, showed initiative and courage when they were called by God to preserve the God-willed line of the Messiah. They are all seen by Matthew as integral to God's plan, and God's unfolding history. Each one of them plays a fundamentally important role at major turning points of the history of God's people:

Tamar — continues Judah's line after the death of Er and Onan (see Genesis 46, 12).
Rahab — the heroine at Jericho, where Israel enters the promised land (see Joshua 2, 1-21; 6, 17-25).

Ruth — the mother of Obed, the grandfather of King David (see Ruth 4, 18-22).
Bathsheba — conceives Solomon by David, and thus the Davidic royal line is continued.
Mary — 'of whom Jesus was born, who is called Christ' (Matthew 1, 16).

Against the prejudices and the head-wagging of contemporary culture and social standards, these women were to be considered as the wonderful instruments of God's plan for mankind. In the case of the Old Testament women, God overcame moral irregularities, and the questionable unions between the human parents. In the case of Mary, something even greater had to be overcome: the complete absence of a father's begetting. The problem is resolved in verse 20:

Joseph, son of David, do not fear to take Mary your wife, for that which is conceived in her is of the Holy Spirit.

It is incorrect to claim that Matthew's infancy narrative does not provide us with a Mariology or a positive view of woman. In fact, despite its being less devoted to the person of Mary than Luke, it provides us with an all-important starting point for our consideration of how the various Gospel traditions carried Jesus' attitudes and teachings into the preaching of the early Church. Mary is presented as the final and perfect instrument in God's providence in continuing, and finally bringing to fruition, the messianic hopes of Israel. These hopes, however, have been marked — from the very beginnings — by women open to God's action in their lives, cost them what it may. Despite all the judgements of men, society and culture, which will forever surround the mystery of woman, they are the ones who most of all were open to the initiative of God working in them. Thus, one of them eventually became the mother of Jesus.

It is precisely this radical openness to the action of God in her life that will become the leitmotif of the Lucan presentation of Mary. There may be differences and even contradictions in the two infancy narratives preserved by Matthew and Luke, and it is generally admitted that the Lucan narrative, dominated by the figure of Mary, has more to tell us about women. However, I would like to suggest that Matthew has done more than Luke for an overall understanding of woman within the context of his infancy narrative. The rest of the narrative is certainly dominated by Joseph, but in 1, 1-17 Matthew has shown that not only 'a woman' (Luke's major thrust) but also 'women' have played a decisive role in the gradual unfolding of God's salvation history, because of their openness to his action in their lives.

MATTHEW 12, 46-50: 'MY BROTHER, AND SISTER, AND MOTHER'[50]

We need now to glance, however briefly, at the use that the Evangelist Matthew makes of Mark 3, 31-35. I am presupposing that Matthew has Mark before him, and if such is the case, then Matthew's slight rewriting of his source becomes important. The two texts can be best appreciated through the following parallel.

Mark 3, 31-35	*Matthew 12, 46-50*
31. And his mother and his brothers came; and standing outside they sent to him and called him.	46. While he was still speaking to the people, behold his mother and his brothers stood outside to speak to him.
32. And a crowd was sitting about him; and they said to him, 'Your mother and your brothers are outside, asking for you.'	
33. And he replied, 'Who are my mother and my brothers?'	48. But he replied to the man who told him, 'Who is my mother and who are my brothers?'
34. And looking around on those who sat about him, he said, 'Here are my mother and my brothers!	49. And stretching out his hand toward his disciples, he said, 'Here are my mother and my brothers!
35. Whoever does the will of God is my brother, and sister, and mother.'	50. For whoever does the will of my Father in heaven is my brother, and sister, and mother.'

There are a few important features in Matthew's rewriting of the Marcan passage that need to be clarified. To start with, Matthew sets up a situation that closely parallels a Jewish school. Notice that Mark's 'crowd' is eliminated, and that the presence of his natural family is communicated to Jesus by a man (v.48) rather than via the crowd. The explanation of the identity of the listeners to Jesus' reply to the presence of his family is also changed. No longer does he 'look around on those who sat about him' (Mark 3, 34a), a generic group, among whom there will be some who do the will of God (v.35). Instead he points directly at the disciples: 'And stretching out his hand towards his disciples' (Matthew 12, 49a).

What follows is a description and an identification of a *disciple of Jesus*. Here we find that Matthew lists male and female, without any sign of division or distinction: disciples are Jesus' mother and brothers and sisters, all doing the will of the one Father:

Here are my mother and my brothers! For whoever does the will of my Father in heaven is my brother, and sister, and mother (12, 49b-50).

Once we realize that Matthew is rewriting Mark we can begin to see the importance of the passage: The Matthean community, all those doing the will of the Father of Jesus, the disciples, men and women without distinction, are the 'new family' of Jesus.

Again we find, even in Matthew, the essential characteristics of any Christian community: 'There is neither male nor female, for you are all one in Christ' (Galatians 3, 28). Christian discipleship can admit of no culturally or historically conditioned barriers.[51]

It has been generally argued that Matthew's perspective leaves little space for a developed theology of 'woman'. The Gospel was clearly written for an audience well-versed in Jewish thought and customs, but Matthew was nevertheless leading them into the wider world of the mission of the Gentiles. This is clear from many passages in the Gospel, but especially in Jesus' parting words to his infant Church:

Go, therefore, and make disciples of all nations (28, 19).

As Matthew builds the bridge between a largely Jewish community and the Gentile world, he shows great love and respect for the ways of Israel, which must not be lost. This also can be found in many places in the Gospel, but especially in some words of Jesus that only Matthew reports, and that may well be a little biographical description of the Evangelist himself:

Every scribe who has been trained for the kingdom of heaven is like a householder who brings out of his treasure what is new and what is old (13, 52)

In this journey from the old to the new, while the ways of Israel are to be loved and respected, the newness of Jesus breaks through unmistakably.[52]

We have already seen that such radical newness was to be found in the way Jesus of Nazareth related to women, and that it stands at the heart of the Pauline Gospel. We now find again that it appears faithfully in Matthew's story of Jesus: all — women and men — are disciples of Jesus (12, 46-50) and women are singled out as outstanding examples of what it means to be a disciple of Jesus: they are open to the ways of God in their lives, cost them what it may (1, 1-17).

THE GOSPEL OF LUKE

I have already mentioned that Matthew 1-2 has the person of Joseph at the center of the birth and infancy of Jesus, and that Mary plays little part. She never appears as the main protagonist in any scene of the narrative. The opposite is the case in Luke 1-2. Mary, the mother of Jesus, dominates the Lucan account, and Joseph seems merely to stand by.[53] As has always been noticed, it is also Luke who pays much more attention to the role of women in the public ministry of Jesus. It is impossible for me to present a detailed examination of the whole of Luke 1-2, where Mary plays such a leading role, or all the passages in the Gospel where women are important. I would like, therefore, to articulate this chapter on the Gospel of Luke in the following fashion:

1. A study of the annunciation, which leads to Mary's radical commitment of faith in her words: 'Be it done unto me according to your word' (1,38).

2. A short analysis of the birth of Jesus, leading to a comment from the Evangelist that has often been trivialized, but which in fact is of great Mariological importance: 'Mary kept all these things, pondering them in her heart' (2, 19).[54]

3. A further section dealing briefly with some of the important scenes from the public ministry of Jesus where women play an important role. I have reserved this section of my reflection till now, as all of this material is found only in Luke, and it helps us to understand better Luke's very personal use of women to preach the message of Jesus of Nazareth.

1. THE ANNUNCIATION: LUKE 1, 26-38

The first thing to notice about the annunciation story is that it is not the only annunciation story in the infancy narratives of Matthew and Luke. There are several of them (see Matthew 1, 20-21; Luke 1, 11-20; 2, 9-15), and *all* of these annunciation stories follow a literary pattern that had its origins in the great annunciation stories of the Old Testament: the annunciation of Ishmael (Genesis 16, 7-12), the annunciation of Isaac (Genesis 17, 1-21), the annunciation of Isaac at Mamre (Genesis 18, 1-12), the annunciation of Samson (Judges 13, 2-21). The pattern is *always* as follows, both in the Old Testament and in the infancy narratives. It is particularly present in Luke 1, 26-38.[55]

1. The appearance of an angel of the Lord (Luke 1, 26-28)
2. Fear when confronted (v.29)
3. The message:
The visionary is addressed (vv. 28, 30)
The visionary is described by the angel (v.28)
He/she is urged not to be afraid (v.31)
A woman is or will be with child (v.31)
She will give birth (v.31)
The child is given a name (v.31)
The child's future is described (vv.32,33,35)
4. An objection is raised and/or a sign is requested (v.34)
5. A sign is given (vv.36-37).

With this pattern clearly in mind we can now briefly examine Luke's special use of it in his presentation of the annunciation of the birth of Jesus of Nazareth. The scene opens with a deliberate link back to the conclusion of the annunciation of John the Baptist. In 1, 24 we read:

After these days his wife Elizabeth conceived, and *for five months* she hid herself.

We then read in verse 26, at the opening of the annunciation of Jesus: '*In the sixth month* the angel Gabriel was sent'. There is a further connection across the two annunciation stories through the name of the angel, as the angel Gabriel was also involved in the annunciation of the birth of John the Baptist to Zechariah (see v.19). There is also a further important reason for the choice of 'the sixth month'. Not only does it look back to the annunciation of John the Baptist, but it also looks forward to the next scene (1, 39-56) where the two mothers meet. Across the whole three narratives (the annunciations to Zechariah and to Mary, and then the meeting of the two mothers) there is always an important link between the two sons. For Luke, it is vital that the reader recognize that John the Baptist was a truly great figure in the history of salvation — but that Jesus was the greatest of all figures. Within his infancy narrative, Luke chooses beautifully to fasten upon the quickening of the infant John within his mother's womb as a sign of salutation of Jesus, still a child being carried in the womb of his mother Mary (see 1, 44). As is well known, it is about the sixth month of pregnancy when this quickening process is particularly felt by a mother.

The angel comes 'to a virgin'. The word 'virgin' appears twice in verse 27, and in this way Luke is indicating that Mary was a virgin at the conception of Jesus. She is described as 'betrothed to a man whose name was Joseph'. This affirmation must be taken seriously. As yet, Mary had not been officially 'led to the house' of Joseph, but her being betrothed to a man explicitly named as 'of the House of David' makes her part of that house, and assures the continuation of the Davidic promise. Notice that there is no indication here of a vow to perpetual virginity, and notice also that the whole of the stress on the virginal aspect of Mary is placed *before* the conception of Jesus. The virginity of Mary, as far as the New Testament is concerned, is not about the virtue of *Mary*, but it is about the *origins of Jesus*. The whole issue of virginity is to assure that Jesus' origins are from God, and that there was no human intervention — with the exception of the unique role of Mary — in the conception of this child. As far as the Gospels are concerned, the virginity of Mary is not a Mariological issue, but a Christological matter of considerable importance. There is no one with even a minimum knowledge of Jewish psychology, and the theological blessedness of a fruitful marriage, based on the command of Jahweh in Genesis 1, 28, who would suggest that a betrothed Jewish girl would have gone into a situation of betrothal after having taken a vow of virginity. We could draw a rough parallel with our own times, as it would be highly unlikely that a young twentieth-century woman would enter into an engagement to marry with the intention of remaining a virgin. The parallel is weak, however, as the first-century Jewish betrothal was a much more serious and binding matter than our twentieth-century engagement. The young girl was formally regarded as the man's wife (see, for example, Matthew 1, 20).

The Old Testament pattern of a birth annunciation begins as the angel greets Mary with the word 'Hail'. However, the Greek behind our tame English translation means 'rejoice', and not far from the surface here are two Old Testament prophecies, which in the Greek translation of the Septuagint use the same verb:

Sing aloud, O daughter of Zion; shout, O Israel!
Rejoice and exult with all your heart,
O daughter of Jerusalem! (Zephaniah 3, 14).
Rejoice heart and soul, daughter of Zion!
Shout with gladness, daughter of Jerusalem!
See now, your king comes to you (Zechariah 9, 9 JB).

The implicit reference to these famous messianic prophecies indicates that the angel's situation is also an invitation to Mary to rejoice at the wonderful advent of the messianic times that are about to happen through her.

This powerful salutation is followed by an address from the angel, calling Mary 'favoured one'. This is the best translation of the original Greek, as it is a passive participle (*kecharitomene*). It is to be preferred to our usual traditional translation, 'full of Grace', although this latter version is not found in any of the modern translations of the New Testament.[56] This expression is not used as an exaltation of someone who is already in possession of the fullness of God's gifts. She is what she is only because of the wonderful privilege that is about to be conferred upon her by God. As is the case throughout this narrative (see also 1, 38 and 48), Mary is described as *receiving* God's great gifts, not as someone who already possesses everything, nor as someone endowed with the power to give Grace. This is important, as some of the enthusiastic devotional approaches to Mary have come dangerously close to suggesting that because of her extraordinary gifts in the order of Grace, God almost *had* to choose her. Such thinking is both biblically and theologically unsound, but it enjoys enormous popularity. Closely linked to such suggestions is the belief that everything in the order of salvation passes through Mary. As well as robbing us of the woman, Mary of Nazareth, these non-biblical ways of understanding her person and her role in salvation history risk a loss of contact with two of the central doctrines of our faith: that everything in the order of salvation is a gift of God (Grace), and that Jesus is the one true mediator of all salvation. To correct these dangerous, but extremely popular views, the Council Fathers at Vatican II wrote beautifully:

In the words of the apostle there is but one mediator: 'for there is but one God and one mediator of God and men, the man Jesus Christ, who gave himself a redemption for all' (1 Timothy 2, 5-6). But Mary's function as mother of men in no way obscures or diminishes this unique mediation of Christ, but rather shows its power. But the Blessed Virgin's salutary influence on men originates *not in any inner necessity but in the disposition of God*. It flows forth from the superabundance of the merits of Christ, rests on his mediation, depends entirely on it and draws all its power from it. (*Lumen Gentium* 60. Stress mine.)

Once we are open to all the implications of this profoundly biblical teaching, reaching right back into the very first interventions of God into the history of mankind, then the phrase of the angel, 'the Lord is with you', can take on its fullest meaning. The expression 'highly favoured one' points out that the divine plan of God has chosen for her a unique role in his history of salvation. She is about to be offered a once-and-for-all, never-to-be-repeated role among men and women. This is *given*; she *receives* — or better, at this stage she is asked if she is prepared to let go of her world and her plans to accept such a role. I said earlier that we must avoid the tendency to impose upon the Lucan story the idea that God *had* to choose Mary; God is always free. It is also important, for a full appreciation, to allow Mary the same freedom! Luke's account makes clear that what took place in and through Mary happened because God deigned to shower his favors upon this girl, and as we shall see, she had the faith and the courage to be receptive to these favors. This makes sense of the next part of the angel's salutation: 'the Lord is with you!' The assurance that the Lord will be with her is a guarantee that the plans that God has for Mary will be effectively realized, depending upon her response to his call.

Although following the Old Testament annunciation pattern, Mary's being troubled and 'considering in her mind what sort of greeting this might be' (v.29) is a natural enough reaction. Yet, even though this 'astonishment' is both a part of a literary pattern and a perfectly understandable natural reaction to such an apparition, there is more to it. Mary's *first* reaction is one of human confusion and puzzlement. She is unable to utter a single word in her shock and consternation. Such a situation is then altered by a further explanation from the angel: 'You have found favour with God (v.30).' We have already seen that all that is about to happen takes place because of God's initiative in having selected this girl called Mary for a tremendous task and role in the history of salvation. The theme is repeated here, as it is further clarified. Something is happening *to* Mary. The expression 'to find favour' reflects an Old Testament turn of phrase (see Genesis 6, 8; Judges 6, 17; 1 Samuel 1, 18; 2 Samuel 15, 25), and it always indicates the free and gracious choice of God who favors particular men and women. The stress is still upon the wonderful mystery of a God of love who chooses one of us; it has nothing to do with someone's human acceptability for such a task.

In verses 31-33 we find the continuation of the Old Testament annunciation pattern. The conception and birth of a wonderful child is announced. Notice that, as yet, nothing has been said of the nature of the conception. In this first moment of the annunciation, the child is described in a way that reflects the classical terms of Jewish messianic hopes:

He will be great,
and will be called
the Son of the Most High;
and the Lord God will give to him

the throne of his father David,
and he will reign over the house of Jacob for ever;
and of his kingdom there will be no end.

Notice the terms used to express *who* this son will be: son of the Most High and son of David. Notice then *what* he will do: he will be great, he will reign over the house of Jacob for ever, his kingdom will have no end. *All* of these expectations can be found in the Jewish hopes for their coming Messiah. This is even the case for the term 'the son of the Most High', which ultimately has its origins in Israel's calling the king (see Psalm 2, 7 and 2 Samuel 7, 14) and the people (see, for example, Hosea 11, 1) a 'son of God'.[57] Mary, therefore, is being told that she will be the mother of the expected Messiah. Although an extraordinary honor is being conferred upon her through the initiative of God, she is still within the realm of something *expected* and *humanly possible*. This leads to verse 34, where Mary poses the question that will give Luke space to announce, through the words of the angel, that this child is something more than the fulfilment of Jewish messianic hopes. Mary now moves away from the puzzled astonishment and fear that met the first greeting of the angel (v.29). She now poses a perfectly sound, reasonable question. She has moved from astonishment to reasonability. Just as Zechariah asked for some explanation of *how* the angelic promise will come true, Mary in her particular set of physical circumstances asks:

How can this be, *since I have no husband?*

Mary's problem arises from the fact that she has no sexual relationship with a man. That the reference is to the sexual union is made amply clear by the use of the present tense of the verb 'to know'. 'Since I know not man' is a good translation, as long as it carries with it the profound biblical idea of the sexual union in the use of the verb 'to know' (see, for example, Genesis 4, 1; 19, 8; Judges 11, 39; 21, 12; 1 Samuel 1, 19). The use of the present tense in the construction makes the sentence rather clumsy, and it must mean: 'I do not have a husband with whom I am having sexual relations'. This present tense is central to the correct interpretation of the whole passage. The angel has said 'You *will* conceive' (v.31), and this could — if read without Mary's query of verse 34 — refer to some future union with Joseph. Mary's reply shows that it is the decision she is to make within this very moment that is to determine such a conception, and at this moment she is a 'virgin' (v.27), and has never had sexual union with her husband. How is such a conception possible at this moment?

Many Catholic scholars have, in the past, argued that verse 34 indicated that Mary was vowed to virginity. They have argued that it means: 'I have resolved not to know a man'. Apart from the strain that this puts upon the Greek of the text itself, it simply does not make sense of the context. What is the point of the betrothal in verse 27 if Mary was already vowed to virginity? Are both Mary and Joseph vowed to such a form of life? There is no indication of such a situation in the text of the Gospel of Luke, no matter how widespread this idea may have become in the early apocryphal legends and in popular piety.[58] In fact, as I have already mentioned, no writer with even a minimum knowledge of Jewish psychology and understanding of the blessedness of a fruitful marriage (and Luke must be credited with at least that much) could have thought of a vow of virginity on the part of a betrothed Palestinian girl in the first century.

We must simply let the story unfold in the way *Luke* tells it. As a background to the whole account, as I have repeatedly indicated, stands the pattern of the Old Testament annunciation stories. Following that pattern, Mary reacts to the angel's message with a query. As I have already indicated, this second reaction from Mary has to be seen as a second stage in her developing journey of faith. She has moved from confusion (v.29) to reason (v.34). Luke uses this second reaction to give himself space for the all-important message about the *how* of this conception: there is to be no human father! In this way we are led into verses 34-35, which tell of the overshadowing of the Holy Spirit, which is the ultimate cause of the child. Once that has been made clear, then we find that Mary's journey of faith comes to its climax. Remember that in verses 32-33 the child was described in terms of a Davidic King, according to the very best of Jewish messianic hopes. Now given the origins of the child, he is further described in a way that outstrips any Jewish expectations: he is described as 'the Son of God' whose conception is the result of the overshadowing of the Holy Spirit:

The Holy Spirit will come upon you,
and the power of the Most High will overshadow you;
therefore the child to be born will be called holy,
the Son of God (v.35).

Still following the annunciation pattern, the 'sign' of Elizabeth is given (v.36), and then, in explanation of what is happening to *both* women, verse 37 announces:

For with God nothing will be impossible.

Notice how carefully Luke has linked both of his annunciation scenes. The physically impossible has happened to Elizabeth — and now the even more impossible has happened to Mary. All that we have read in Luke 1, 5-36 is quite impossible, yet with God nothing is impossible. As I have been indicating throughout the whole of my interpretation of this passage, the wonders that are being described all have their source and sense in God. The text is not primarily an exaltation of the great virtue of a Jewish girl: it is about the transforming power of a great and loving God who can raise up the lowly (see 1, 51).

Now we are in a position to understand Mary's famous words in verse 38:

Behold I am the handmaid of the Lord;
let it be to me according to your word.

The appearance of an angel has led to amazed puzzlement; the annunciation of the birth of a long-awaited Jewish messiah has led to a perfectly logical objection; but in this final stage the angel has shown that Mary has been caught up in a plan of God that reaches outside human measurement and control. She is being asked to give herself and her future history to 'the Holy Spirit . . . the power of the Most High'. She *could* have remained in the realm of the controllable, and baulked at such a suggestion. Instead she commits herself to the ways of God in a consummate act of faith. All that we have seen so far leads up to this profound indication of the reason for Mary's greatness: she is a woman radically open to the presence of God in her life.

There is a further scene in Luke's Gospel that must help us in our understanding of Mary, in the light of what we have just seen. In Luke 8, 19-21 we read:

Then his mother and his brothers came to him, but they could not reach him for the crowd. And he was told, 'Your mother and your brothers are standing outside, desiring to see you'. But he said to them, 'My mother and my brothers are those who hear the word of God and do it'.

As we have already seen in our comparison of Mark 3, 31-35 and Matthew 12, 46-50, for Mark those who 'do the will of God' (Mark 3, 36) *replace* the natural family of Jesus, to form a new 'family of God'. A similar idea is found in Matthew's rewriting of his Marcan source. This is not the case in Luke's Gospel. For Luke, Mary, the mother of Jesus, is the first and most wonderful of all believers. She is the one *par excellence*, who hears the word of God and does it. We have just seen this happen in 1, 26-38. Mary has come face to face, in the annunciation story, with the mystery of God at work within her. Her obedient and enthusiastic acceptance of this unfathomable mystery as God's humble handmaid makes her the first of all believers. She, above all, is the one who 'hears the word of God and does it', and so Luke has made this clear in 8, 19-21, as he corrected any misinterpretation that Mark 3, 31-35 may have made possible, if he had simply repeated what Mark had written.

Mary, before any other person in the whole of the story of Jesus, shows that the wonder of life comes from the acceptance of the active presence of God among us. Thus, she herself provides us with the best interpretation of the annunciation story when she later cries out in her *Magnificat:*

He who is mighty has done great things for me,
and holy is his name (1, 49).

2. MARY AT THE BIRTH OF JESUS: LUKE 2, 1-20

We are all so familiar with the Lucan Christmas story that there may be more to it than is commonly understood. As we have already seen from our analysis of 1, 26-38, the Evangelist Luke is a very skilful writer, capable of communicating profound truths through his use of narrative, his gentle allusions to Old Testament background, and his challenge to Christians of all times. Such is also the case with his story of the birth of Jesus (Luke 2, 1-20).

The account opens (2, 1-7) with the careful presentation of three characters or sets of characters:

(a) The Emperor Augustus, the most famous and respected of all the Roman Emperors because he established a lasting peace throughout the whole Empire that was never again achieved (v.1).

(b) The governor Quirinius, another Roman authority, who ruled over and established order in a smaller region of the Empire. His dates are hard to fit into the Jesus story, but for Luke it is important that a significant Roman authority be mentioned by name (v.2).

(c) Joseph, Mary and a child born on a journey, as there was no room for them at the resting place. The child is laid in a manger and wrapped in swaddling cloths.

Notice the descending order of importance: from the 'great ones' of this world (the Emperor) through his envoys (Quirinius) to the 'little ones' (Joseph, Mary and their son). Yet the reader knows that the real author of peace is not Augustus, the true 'great one' is the child. Notice further that Luke insists on the importance of the swaddling cloths and the fact that he is laid in a manger. After mentioning it in verse 7, he uses these 'signs' for the shepherds in verses 12 and 16. In the whole of the Old Testament there is only one other reference to swaddling cloths — linen bandages wrapped tightly around the limbs of an infant to ensure that his or her limbs will grow strong and straight. It is found in Wisdom 7, 4-5 where Solomon, a great Davidic King, is presented as writing of his own birth:

I was carefully swaddled and nursed,
for no king has any other way
to begin at birth (AT).

The swaddling cloths are a symbol of the newly born Davidic King! Jesus! Being laid in a manger is also a sign and symbol of what is to come. This child in a manger, soon to be visited by shepherds, has established a situation among men and women where an ancient lament of Jahweh to his people can now be reversed:

I reared sons, I brought them up,
but they have rebelled against me.
The ox knows its owner,
and the ass *its master's manger.*
Israel knows nothing,
my people understands nothing (Isaiah, 1, 2-3 AT).

In the second scene (vv.8-14) the reversal of the Isaian lamentation takes place through the shepherds. They are also 'little people', not regarded very highly by the paragons of religious perfection, as they tended to be involved in petty thieving, and they led their flocks into other people's pastures. Yet, it is to them that the heavenly message comes, a message of

A babe wrapped in swaddling cloths and lying in a manger (2, 12)

who would bring peace to humankind, if they would but be prepared to receive what he has come to bring (v.14).

In the third scene (vv.15-20), all the protagonists from verses 1-7 and 8-14 are assembled, as the shepherds come to find Mary and Joseph with the child (v.16). Their decision to do this flows directly from their belief that what has been revealed to them comes from God:

Let us go over to Bethlehem and see this thing that has happened, which the Lord has made known to us (v.15).

Thus they come to Bethlehem, find the child in the manger, and tell of all the wonderful things that have been made known to them (vv. 16-17). The passage then concludes with a final dramatic presentation of three different reactions to the new-born King and Messiah in the skilfully written verses 18-20. This passage, in three very short remarks, tells us about the reactions of:

(a) 'All who heard of it' (v.18).

(b) Mary (v.19).

(c) The shepherds (v.20).

Notice how Luke has placed the figure of Mary at the center of this threefold reaction to the birth. By doing this he wants to call the particular attention of the reader to her reaction, in comparison with the reaction of 'all who heard it', which comes before, and of the shepherds, which comes after. Those two reactions form a sort of frame around the reaction of Mary, and thus throw it into greater relief. Let us analyze briefly the reactions of the two groups, which flank the central reaction of Mary. We will then be in a better position to understand fully what Luke wishes to tell his readers in verse 19.

The reaction of 'all who heard' is one of astonishment (v.18). There is no reference to faith, and there is no mention of any desire to go and see the child, in contrast to the desire of the shepherds to do just that. At the wonders surrounding the birth of John the Baptist there was a similar reaction — 'And they all marvelled' (1, 63) — but the marvelling led them further in that case: 'and all who heard them laid them up in their hearts' (1, 66). There is no such reaction at the birth of Jesus. As I have already mentioned, Luke is most concerned that the reader see that there is a close relationship between John the Baptist and Jesus, but that Jesus is the greater of the two because he is the fruit of the overshadowing of the Holy Spirit, the power of the Most High (1, 35). In this case, 'all who heard it' have made a wrong choice. There are no indications that their marvelling at the birth of Jesus led them to treasure these things in their hearts. Clearly, all we have here is wonder; it is only Mary who will treasure these things in her heart (v.19).

The reaction of the shepherds is to go back to their flocks, not making it known any further, but glorifying and praising God who has accomplished such great things. They are certainly the forerunners of future believers who will glorify God for what they have heard and will praise God for what they have seen (v.20). There has now begun a praise and glory of God on earth, echoing the praise and glory of God by the heavenly host (see vv.13-14). Having made this point, the shepherds disappear from the Gospel story. They are not about when Jesus begins his public ministry. Luke, like Matthew, who had to send the Magi back home (see Matthew 2, 12), could not have Jesus preaching, from his very first moments, to an already enthusiastic group of believers who had come to faith at his birth — shepherds and others who may have heard the news, and followed the career of this baby as he grew into manhood! This had to be avoided because historically Jesus' public preaching simply was not received in that way. Therefore, the shepherds make their final exit in verse 20, never to be seen or heard of again.

There is one figure, however, who does bridge the gap between the infancy narrative and the stories of the ministry of Jesus: Mary, the mother of Jesus. She is the only adult mentioned in Luke 1-2 who reappears in the body of the Gospel. We must understand verse 19, continuing what we have already learnt from the annunciation story, as the preparatory presentation of the Mary who will reappear in the Gospel story, and at the beginning of the Acts of the Apostles, Luke's second volume. Luke 2, 19 reads:

But Mary kept all these things, pondering them in her heart.

At the conclusion of Luke's infancy narrative, after the finding of the boy Jesus in the Temple, and after what can only be understood as a gentle reprimand:

How is it that you sought me? Did you not know that I must be in my Father's house? (2, 49).

Again we read:

And they did not understand the saying which he spoke to them . . . and his mother kept all these things in her heart (2, 50-51).

A correct interpretation of these passages is vital for an understanding of the Lucan presentation of Mary. We must again avoid some of the reflections that have been motivated by purely pious speculation, as again there is a profoundly biblical background and meaning involved. Even more important, we must also reject any use of these passages as 'proof' for the argument that Mary observed all of these events carefully and stored them away, so that she could later tell them to Luke, or to someone who eventually passed the stories on to Luke. This is a position still adopted by some more conservative scholars in an attempt to secure the historicity (in the twentieth-century sense of that word) of the narrative. This sort of reasoning — seeking after 'facts' rather than inspired 'truth' — is a trivialization of a very important Lucan theological argument, and a reduction of the historical Mary to the near-blasphemous parody of the Evangelists in the last supper scene from *Jesus Christ Superstar:*

Always hoped that I'd be an apostle.
Knew that I would make it if I tried.
Then when we retire we can write the Gospels,
so they'll still talk about us when we've died.

That sort of argument — applied to Mary through an incorrect reading of the Lucan text — simply will not do!

The expression 'to keep something in the heart', or better, as the Jerusalem Bible translates it, 'to treasure something in the heart', is closely linked to an Old Testament expression. It is found throughout the books of the Old Testament (see Genesis 37, 11; 1 Samuel 2, 13; Malachi 2, 2) but it is especially important in the Wisdom literature (see Sirach 39, 1-3; Proverbs 31; Psalm 119, 11) and the Apocalyptic literature (see Daniel 1, 8; 4, 28; 7, 28). The idea that comes to Luke from the biblical tradition is closely connected to a situation where a mere human has some sort of experience or receives some sort of revelation that has its origins in God. This experience or revelation is beyond the ken of the recipient, but there is some sort of mysterious significance that, as yet, he or she cannot fully penetrate. In such a situation one can marvel, and then go one's way, as we found in the reaction of 'all who heard' in verse 18. However, according to the biblical tradition, the man or woman of faith, despite an inability to understand what he or she has seen, heard, or both, does not reject the incomprehensible. The revelation of the event is 'treasured', taken into the deepest recesses of one's being, guarded and pondered over within the depths of one's heart. The faithful one simply awaits some time in God's future, a moment that will be determined by God's plan and God's history, when the whole truth will be revealed in all its fullness.

This is Mary's situation. Angels from heaven have appeared to her, she has become the mother of the Son of God through the overshadowing of the Holy Spirit, and shepherds have come from the fields with a message of heavenly revelations and choirs of angels. As we have already seen in our analysis of the annunciation story, all of this was well beyond anything Mary could control or understand.

How can this be? (1, 34).

The same perplexity is repeated in the finding of Jesus in the Temple:

They did not understand the saying which he spoke to them (2, 50).

Never in these beautiful accounts is Mary presented as a woman in control of all that is happening to her, fully aware of all the consequences of the pattern of life that her response to God will create for her. However, in faith, what has been revealed to her has been 'treasured', as she awaits the fullness of God's revelation to her. Already in 1, 38 she has simply opened herself to the power of God's word:

Be it done unto me according to your word.

Then, in her *Magnificat*, she shows that she has no illusions over the source of all that has been done to her and for her — and consequently for 'all generations':

He has regarded the low estate of his handmaiden.
For behold, henceforth all generations will call me blessed;
For he who is mighty has done great things for me,
And holy is his name (1, 48-49).

The rest of the *Magnificat* (vv.51-55) shows, moreover, wherein lies the source of her preparedness to respond in such a fashion: she has learnt from the story of her people, from the patriarchs down to her own time, that the God of Israel always has (and always will):

put down the mighty from their thrones
and exalted those of low degree (v.52).

This is the portrait of Mary that comes to us from the Lucan infancy narrative: a woman who has been called from among us to a unique greatness. Yet her greatness lies in the fact that she is, above all, a woman of faith. The girl from Nazareth could not possibly be expected to understand the depths of the mystery that was being revealed to her, a mystery in which she was to play an indispensable role: the giver of the flesh and blood in the mystery of the Incarnation. How all this could be, and why it should happen to her, she could not understand; but as mother of all believers—of all of us caught up in the same wonderful mystery of God's ways in our lives —she compromised herself *in faith*, as she 'treasured all these things and pondered over them in her heart' (Luke 2, 19, 51. J.B.)

The story does not end there. As I have already mentioned, Mary is the only adult character from Luke 1-2 who reappears in the ministry of Jesus. Mary's two appearances in the Gospel proper show that she has indeed treasured what has been revealed to her, and that she continues as the mother of all believers, open to the word at work in her. Luke deliberately presents her as the model of the faithful one.

As we have already seen in 8, 19-21 we hear of the criteria for membership of the new family of faith that Jesus is gathering around himself:

Now there came to him his mother and his brothers, but they were not able to reach him on account of the crowd. It was announced to him, 'Your mother and your brothers are standing outside, wishing to see you'. But he replied and said to them, 'My mother and my brothers are those who hear the word of God and do it'.

Mary has led the way in this, and thus becomes not only the mother of Jesus, but the mother of all who take the risk of hearing the word of God and doing it.

The final passage from the Gospel where Jesus' mother is called into question makes the same point in a very telling way:

And it happened while he was saying these things that a woman from the crowd, raising her voice, said to him, 'Blessed is the womb that bore you, and the breasts you sucked'. But he said, 'No, blessed are those who hear the word of God and keep it' (11, 27-28. A.T.).

It is perhaps unfortunate that a great part of the traditional devotion to Mary has not listened more carefully to this encounter between Jesus and this woman who calls out from the crowd. Most would find themselves on the side of the woman, and against Jesus. We have traditionally placed the greatness of Mary in her physical attributes, in her virginity, in the blessed womb that carried the Savior, and her body, which nourished him. These attributes have their place and their importance, but Jesus insists that we place the greatness of Mary where all true greatness in a Christian disciple must be found: in her hearing the word of God and in her keeping it. If the annunciation scene had gone a little differently, and the angel had commanded 'Go, conceive a child by Joseph and he shall be the Son of God', Mary would have certainly been just as perplexed, and caught in a mystery that she could not fathom. If, in the midst of that mystery she had still replied 'Be it done unto me according to your word', and the Christian story, as we know it, had unfolded from such a beginning — would Mary have been any less a figure in the history of salvation? This is an important question, which readers of this book need to answer in the light of Luke 11, 27-28. As you wonder at the person and role of Mary of Nazareth among us, whose side do you stand on — the woman from the crowd: 'Blessed is the womb that bore you, and the breasts you sucked' — or Jesus: 'No, blessed are those who hear the word of God and keep it'?

As Mary herself has told us, her greatness did not lie in her being the physical mother of Jesus. That was only the *consequence* of her being committed to a radical life of faith. She herself predicted: 'All generations will call me *blessed*' (1,48). Now we know why:

Blessed are those who hear the word of God and keep it (11, 28).

It is Mary who, in the infancy stories, is the first to come to faith, and can be rightly called the first of all disciples. We have just seen that during the ministry of Jesus she is presented as the model of a disciple, the 'new family' of Jesus, radically open to the word of God, and prepared to take the risk of living by it. However, even here the story has not yet come to its final conclusion. Mary is presented on those two occasions during the public ministry of Jesus (8, 19-21 and 11, 27-28) as a model of the faithful one, as an outstanding figure of discipleship, but she is, therefore, still living by faith, she is still 'treasuring' the revelation that has been confided to her. The ultimate revelation of the fullness of the mystery still lies in the future.

It is nowadays universally accepted that Luke wrote a two-volume work, as the Gospel runs into the Acts of the Apostles. It is sufficient to read the prologues to each book to see that this is clearly the case (see Luke 1, 1-4 and Acts 1, 1-2). Mary is still present as the Acts of the Apostles opens. After Jesus' resurrection and ascension, she is with the nascent Church, interpreting ever more clearly the mysteries that have been revealed to her. It is for this reason that, at the beginning of Acts, as the earliest Christian community is reported gathering in the upper room to receive the gift of the Spirit of Pentecost, Mary makes her final appearance:

All these with one accord devoted themselves to prayer, together with Mary the mother of Jesus (Acts 1, 14).

This is an indication that for Mary, as for all the disciples gathered there, at Pentecost the Spirit of Truth makes sense and gives direction for all the 'treasured' mysteries — at last! In Luke 1-2 she became the first and the most wonderful of all believers, plunging forward into a darkness of human foolishness, lit up only by her faith in her God, her body 'quickened' by the Holy Spirit, the power of the Most High (see 1, 35), prepared to live entirely by his word (see 1, 38). During the public life of Jesus (8, 19-21 and 11, 27-28) she is again presented as a model of faith, as one who hears the word of God and keeps it. Both of these passages in the Gospel, however, use Jesus' mother within the context of what it means to 'belong' to Jesus, to be a member of the new family of God, gathered around Jesus, prepared to live as he lived. At the beginning of the story of the Church in the

Acts of the Apostles we find a hint that this primacy in the order of faith also placed her in a special position in the Church's earliest days. As yet, in Luke's two volumes, it is only a hint, as she is explicitly mentioned by name in the midst of the earliest community, waiting for its empowering, its divine mandate, to reach out and 'to teach about the Lord Jesus quite openly and unhindered' (Acts 28, 31). We will see that the Fourth Gospel takes this theme further, as Mary becomes the 'mother of the disciple' and the Mother of the Church.

This fairly detailed analysis of these famous and beautiful 'woman' texts makes it clear that for Luke a woman has the primacy in the order of faith. In so far as we can speak of a *history* of salvation, it is a woman who is both chronologically and qualitatively *the first* among those who believe.[59]

3. SOME UNIQUELY LUCAN TEXTS ON WOMEN FROM JESUS' MINISTRY

I wish to glance at some of the special Lucan material that deals with women. It appears to me that what has been said of Mary in the infancy narratives spills over into the women characters used by Luke throughout his story of Jesus' ministry. It is important to understand from the outset that I am devoting this section of our study to material that is found only in Luke. Luke, who is using Mark's Gospel as one of his sources, has taken over the Marcan stories where women play an important role. He further reworks them in a fashion that often betrays his special interest in the theme of women. We will not be examining these passages, although they have occasionally been mentioned in my chapter on Jesus of Nazareth.[60] I am using the material that is only found in Luke. The fact that our Evangelist has chosen to use these particular stories, which no other Evangelist has, indicates that they were of particular importance for him, and they will help us better to appreciate Luke's understanding of the role of women in Jesus' ministry.[61]

THE WIDOW OF NAIN: LUKE 7, 11-17

Luke's story of the raising from the dead of the only son of the widow of Nain follows his account of the curing of a centurion's slave (7, 1-10). The centurion's conversation with Jesus not only emphasized the authority of Jesus, but showed that Jesus' authority was respected by people other than Jews. It also shows that Jesus' merciful healing reaches outside the limits of Judaism, and outside the limits imposed by Jewish thought and practice. In 7, 11-17, when Jesus raises the widow's only son, the Evangelist reports of the Jewish onlookers: 'fear seized them all' (v.16) in the face of such authority and such daring. He put his hand on the bier and the bearers stood still (v.14). Jesus commands: 'Young man, I tell you to get up', and the 'dead man sat up' (v.15). To perform this miracle Jesus has, in the detail that I have just picked out, broken through further Jewish laws, this time through the laws of uncleanness, but no one dares to question his authority. The only basis for this extraordinary authority is his word. What is missed by many interpreters, however, is that here Jesus shows deep concern over a woman (see v. 13), and he again shatters both Jewish custom and all contemporary understanding of womanhood by moving towards her and performing the miracle entirely without solicitation, or any request marked by faith. Not only are laws of uncleanness in dealing with the dead smashed by Jesus' authority, but also all 'proper' attitudes to the place of a woman, especially a widow, are ended by that same authority.

It is well known that Luke's Gospel is dominated by an idea of salvation history that sees Jesus as the perfect fulfilment of the Scriptures. Here a woman plays a vital role. In displaying his authority, and at the same time, his compassionate movement towards a woman, Jesus is working through acts similar to certain Old Testament stories, such as the account of Elijah and the widow of Zaraphath (1 Kings 17, 23). Luke, in this account, shows that progression and perfection of the prophetic presence in the actions of Jesus, this time through a woman.

A WOMAN WASHES JESUS' FEET: LUKE 7, 36-50

This story is preceded by Jesus' reprimanding the people of his time, and also criticizing the much-respected Pharisees. Thus Luke 7, 34 is a most suitable introduction to the story of Jesus and the woman reputed to be a sinner:

The Son of Man has come eating and drinking; and you say, 'Behold a glutton and a drunkard, a friend of tax-collectors and sinners'.

In the passage itself we again see Jesus, not only prepared to mix with women, but with a sinful woman. She is a woman caught in a situation of perpetual ritual impurity, but with Jesus, cultural prejudices are done away with. He does not send her away, as his host would like (see v.39), but he accepts her ministrations.[62] This meeting between Jesus and the woman betrays a two-way love. Jesus is showing his love by allowing the woman to continue to wash his feet and remain with him, as I have just indicated. On the other hand, the woman shows her love, a love that reflects faith, and the great Marian theme begins to reappear: it is a woman who shows a primacy in the area of love and faith, over against Simon, whom one would expect to be superior in this area.

This point leads us directly into the much-discussed verse 47:

Therefore I tell you, her sins, which are many, are forgiven, for she loved so much; but he who is forgiven little, loves little.

The discussion over this verse has largely been over the use of the past tense (Greek aorist tense) in the expression 'for she loved much'. Speculation sometimes leads preachers and writers to speak of the long antecedent love of this woman, which has eventually produced forgiveness for her. Applications are made to the spiritual life on that basis. However, verse 47 must be understood *within its own immediate context*. From verse 44 onward Jesus is speaking to Simon, the Pharisee. In a series of contrasts he shows how all the signs of love have been lacking in Simon, yet so powerfully present in the woman: footwashing, kissing and anointing. As Jesus turns to forgive the woman she is presented as a model of how one is to relate to Jesus, over against the self-righteousness of the religious authority, who is disgusted that Jesus would allow a ritually unclean person to come near him and then touch him in such an intimate way. The past tense of the verb refers simply to all the events that have just taken place in the house of Simon. The immediate past now produces a present:

Your sins are forgiven (v.48).

As his table companions wonder at his authority (v.49), the scene concludes in a further affirmation of the woman's love and faith in verse 50:

Your faith has saved you; go in peace.

There can be little doubt that here the Evangelist is deliberately setting the loving openness of the woman in sharp contrast to the priggish pride of the self-righteous men.[63]

THE WOMEN WHO ACCOMPANY JESUS — AND WITNESS
TO HIS RESURRECTION: LUKE 8, 1-3; 23, 49-24, 11

Here the Evangelist picks up his all-important journey motif. As
Jesus journeys on his God-directed way he is accompanied by

some women who had been healed of evil spirits and infirmities (8, 2).[64]

That women were actually travelling with Jesus and the Twelve
further substantiates that neither Jesus' message nor his person can
be restricted: women are not to be 'out of it' for any cultural reason.
This cultural question is well covered by Luke, as he indicates that
most of the them come from culturally questionable backgrounds:
'healed of evil spirits and infirmities'. They are just as important as
the Twelve in the hearing of Jesus' word, and being with him as he
journeys along his way. To have their names listed (vv.2-3) also
shows that Luke is concerned to indicate that they are important and
remembered disciples of Jesus. Also worthy of note is the expression
'who provided for them [some manuscripts have 'him'] out of their
means' (v.3). These women have been given physical and spiritual
health by the intervention of Jesus in their lives (v.2), but they now
turn to him and to the other disciples with their material resources. In
some way, Luke is showing that Jesus *depends* upon the help of
women, and at the end of the Gospel, this help shifts away from the
material into the urgent mission of spreading the good news of the
risen Christ (23, 49-24, 11).
  Although the basic message of the presence of women at the tomb
of Jesus has alrady been discussed,[65] there are some important Lucan
variations upon this basic event that need to be noticed. In 23, 49 it is
the very same group of women, whose names are repeated, who are
present at the Cross, the burial and the empty tomb of Jesus: 'the
women who followed him from Galilee' (23, 49-55). There is a
clearly designed purpose in the Lucan use of these women. This same
group of women 'journeys' with him, both physically and spiritually,
from Galilee to Jerusalem, and through all the Paschal events that
take place in that city. The disciples disappear, with the exception of
Judas and Peter — both of whom fail Jesus — after the Garden at
Gethsemane. It is only the women who are with Jesus from Galilee to
Calvary (23, 49), to the burial (23, 55), and into the experiences of
Easter Day (24, 1 and 10), and Luke takes care to mention that fact
on each occasion. They became the first witnesses to the resurrection
of Jesus (24, 1-11). The following and the caring for the pre-Easter
Jesus lead them to be the first to proclaim the Easter message:

Returning from the tomb they told all this to the eleven and to all the rest (24, 9).

Interestingly enough, the incipient Easter faith of the women is met by hardness of heart from the men:

But these words seemed to them an idle tale, and they did not believe them (24, 11).

Again we seem to be in touch with a Lucan association of women with the history of salvation. They are there from the start (8, 1-3) and they are witnesses to the resurrection (24, 1-11). According to Acts 1, 21-22 this would qualify them for candidacy for the vacant position of the twelfth apostle! Central to the Lucan resurrection account, of course, is the story of the journey to Emmaus (24, 13-35). In that account two male disciples, one named Cleopas and the other unnamed,

were going to a village named Emmaus, about seven miles *away from* Jerusalem (24, 13. A.T.).

Given the centrality of the Lucan theme of a journey *to* Jerusalem, the Paschal events that happen *in* Jerusalem, and the beginnings of the Church *in* Jerusalem before the nascent Church sets out 'to all the nations' (24, 47) and 'to the end of the earth' (Acts 1, 8), these *men* must be seen as walking out of salvation history, as they walk '*away from*' Jerusalem. Jesus himself must touch them with his word (vv.25-27 and 32) and his Sacrament (vv.28-30). And then:

they rose that same hour and *returned to Jerusalem* (v.33).

Full of their experience, they find that *in Jerusalem* this message is already being proclaimed:

The Lord has risen indeed, and has appeared to Simon (v.34).

Behind this, one can almost sense a Lucan comment: this was the message already proclaimed to the men by the women 'who had followed him from Galilee' (24, 49-55). They had proclaimed the message consigned to them by the angel:

Remember how he told you, *while he was still in Galilee,* that the Son of Man must be delivered into the hands of sinful men, and be crucified, and on the third day rise (24, 6-7).

Luke tells us that the women *did* remember those words, and that they told the eleven (see 8, 1-2: the 'eleven' were also 'in Galilee'), who seem to have forgotten. Not only have they forgotten, but

These words seemed to them an idle tale and they did not believe them (24, 11).

The whole of the Lucan Easter story has a subtle sub-theme throughout: against the background of the disbelief of disciples, women are the *first* to come to Easter faith and the *first* to proclaim it. We are again in touch with a chronological and qualitative primacy of faith.

MARTHA AND MARY: LUKE 10, 38-42

The Martha and Mary episode has long been a passage used to show the superiority of a contemplative, prayer-filled life, over against an active one.[66] If we read this account without any relation to its immediate context, that is its obvious meaning. However, as I have pointed out on several occasions, each passage must be read in its literary context, and a determining feature of any interpretation of the Martha and Mary episode must be that it immediately follows the parable of the Good Samaritan (see Luke 10, 25-37). This parable is told in reply to a self-righteous lawyer who, when forced to admit that he must love his neighbor to 'inherit eternal life' (vv.25-28), wishes 'to justify himself' through the discussion of a point of law: 'Who is my neighbour?' (v.29).

Through the parable of the Good Samaritan Jesus demonstrates that 'love to God and neighbour is in itself the life of the heavenly kingdom, already begun on earth',[67] and that true disciples of Jesus do not limit themselves to obeying laws, but actively seize upon opportunities to love anyone who claims their love. The lawyer is then challenged:

Go and do likewise (10, 37).

So far so good, but that is not the whole story. As well as the active 'reaching out', which is so important (and perhaps easier to perform for the aggressive male), there is another side to the medal.

While active love of neighbor is one aspect of discipleship (vv.25-37), the story of Martha and Mary (vv.38-42) goes one step further, showing Luke's readers that listening to Jesus' word is also a fundamental element in discipleship.

When speaking to Martha, Jesus is giving a proper perspective to true hospitality among friends. The physical preparation of the meal and the listening are *both* important aspects of service, but neither must become a *problem*. Martha's mistake is not that she is caring for her guest's physical needs. That was what the Good Samaritan did in the immediately previous parable. The difficulty is that she is 'anxious and troubled about many things' (v.41). She is thus losing touch with the direction and purpose of all that she is doing. We must take care to read the story of the Good Samaritan and the story of Martha and Mary *together*. What Martha is doing in her story is repeating what has been praised in the parable of the Good Samaritan. However, there is more to discipleship than active caring — there must also be a passive listening to the word of Jesus and a preparedness to live by it. We have seen that this was the hallmark of the greatness of Mary. *Both* 'listening' and 'keeping' are necessary, but again there is a question of primacy, and here there can be no illusions. Good deeds are nothing more than good deeds unless they are nourished by a sitting at the Lord's feet, listening to his teaching (v.39). It is here that all good deeds find their source and their purpose. Again we are dealing with the primacy of a preparedness to let all go, to wait for the profound transformation that can come about through the presence, the person and the word of Jesus. This is the 'good portion' that Mary has chosen. Again, Luke has a woman showing the way!

THE CURE OF THE CRIPPLED WOMAN: LUKE 13, 10-17

Scholars always point out that the uniquely Lucan story of the healing of the crippled woman in the synagogue is a clumsy insertion at this stage of Luke's journey narrative, which runs from 9, 51 to 19, 44. It is clumsy both because it is a miracle story, while most of the journey narrative is made up of teaching material, and because it seems to disturb the logic of the passage.[68] It is precisely the 'maverick' nature of the passage that indicates that it is important to the Evangelist; he therefore inserted it here, no matter what it did to his journey narrative construction, because he has something important to say through this miracle story.

Again several critical issues become clear. Jesus breaks the Law and cuts through all canons of Jewish male behavior as he cures on a Sabbath, and he reaches out to cure the woman (as he did with the widow of Nain) without any request or sign of faith from the woman herself (vv.12-13). The first point to notice, therefore, is Jesus' solicitude for the woman. He really cares. G. B. Caird has suggested that Jesus is 'acting in obedience to a necessity which takes prece-

72

dence over all other obligations, including the Sabbath law'.[69] Jesus then answers the usual criticism from his hard-headed male audience by asking if it is unreasonable to be more merciful to an animal than to another human being, a subtle criticism of their attitude to women, so much at variance with his own (vv.15-16). By praising God, the woman shows that the cure has created faith (v.13). She has recognized the source of her cure, a miracle that has resulted from love rather than obedience to the Law. Luke has placed this passage within this context deliberately. He will now show Jesus in conflict with the children of Isaac, Abraham and Jacob (vv.22-30: see v.28) and with the Pharisees (vv.31-35), having already shown his readers where Jesus stands—on the side of love rather than on the side of Law. As this is the case, it is very important to notice that this action from Jesus on behalf of the women leads to a reaction from 'all the people':

And all the people rejoiced at the glorious things that were done by him (v.17).

Jesus is not only a man of words, like the teachers in Israel, but also a doer of glorious deeds. The miracle story of 13, 10-17 is certainly not out of place, and again Luke has chosen a woman to show how his deeds can create faith — within the context of the hardness and disbelief of men.

It is difficult, and perhaps dangerous, to attempt to pick out some overarching motifs from this analysis of some of the special material where women play an important role. More could be said, and indeed there are two uniquely Lucan parables that have women at their center: the lost coin (15, 8-10) and the importunate widow's approach to the unjust judge (19, 1-8). Along with all the material that we have examined so far, they add to the impression that women played an important role in the Lucan communities.[70] However rash it may be, it seems unavoidable that one must conclude that, in the first place, 'the woman', Mary, is presented as the first of all believers and as the model of the faithful one. Secondly, many of the stories about women throughout the Gospel strike the same themes, and they add even more:
(a) All the legal and cultural conditioning that surrounded womanhood must be eliminated, as she is just as important as man in being a hearer of the word, a companion of Jesus on his way, and the recipient of his powerful, forgiving and curing presence. As Eugene Maly has recently written: 'It is not another natural vision of social ethics that Luke has in mind, but a vision which transcends natural categories'.[71] Yet again we are close to the insistence we touched in

the life and attitudes of Jesus, and that we found at the heart of the Pauline Gospel, that 'in Christ' there is neither male nor female, as all are one (see Galatians 3, 28).

(b) Luke has another point to make that picks up, in the experience of these women, the model of Mary. As we have seen, they are often presented as being both chronologically and qualitatively 'first' in the order of faith. This has been seen in their coming to faith while men stand by watching Jesus critically. It is particularly important for the woman in Luke's resurrection account. This primacy in the area of faith — so much a part of the Lucan theology of women — will be developed even further in the Johannine material.

THE APOCALYPSE

The book of the Apocalypse is a notoriously difficult work to understand. Written some time late in the first century, probably in the 90s, by an Elder called 'John' (see 1,1; 4,9; 21,2; 22,8), it is one of the few New Testament books that reveals the name of its author. From there on, however, things are somewhat more complicated! This is because John has used an apocalyptic literary form, taking it from the many examples of this form of literature that flowered in late Judaism, but adapting it to his purpose and message. This leaves the twentieth-century reader with a problem, because apocalyptic literature tends to speak a 'hidden language', using symbols and scenarios whose meaning may have been immediately obvious to first-century readers, well-versed in this sort of book, but which are generally very remote from our contemporary forms of literature. It could also be argued that these first-century apocalyptic documents also reflect an experience of God and his ways in the world that is very different from our own, although one can sense — in the headlong rush into nuclear madness that is so much a part of Western culture and politics today — that we may be heading for a new 'apocalyptic age'!

One of the many puzzles in the Apocalypse, and one that must concern us here, is the famous 'sign in heaven' of Apocalypse 12,1:

A woman clothed with the sun, with the moon under her feet, and on her head a crown of twelve stars.

This woman then plays a major role in the rest of chapter 12. Most readers will be familiar with the popular interpretation of 'the woman' as Mary, the mother of Jesus, an interpretation largely determined by the apparent splendor of the description of verse 1, followed immediately by verse 2:

She was with child and she cried out in her pangs of birth, in anguish for delivery.

There is then a further description of the child in verse 5, and this is generally taken to refer to his being the Messiah:

75

She brought forth a male child, one who is to rule all the nations with a rod of iron.

Nevertheless, even though these pieces of evidence have often led readers to understand the woman as a symbol of Mary, there have been many other suggestions over the centuries, especially that she stands for Israel or the Church.[72]

It appears to me that none of these traditional interpretations does justice to the evidence of the whole of the chapter, and they fail to recognize that 'woman' symbols do not cease with chapter 12. There is another important woman in chapters 17-18 — the great harlot in the desert, mounted on the beast (see 17,1-6) — and still another in chapter 21 — the spouse of the Lamb, united with him on a high mountain, the holy city of the New Jerusalem (see 21,9-11). Is it possible that John's use of 'woman' throughout the second part of his book is deliberate?[73] If there is a deliberate choice of a 'woman' symbol through the last part of the Apocalypse, then this strange work has something important to say on the theme of woman in the New Testament.

I will devote most of my attention to the woman in Apocalypse 12, and then attempt to show how the other two uses of woman symbolism carry further John's argument in Apocalypse 17-18 and 21.[74] This chapter opens the longest subsection of the work, devoted to the pouring out of the seven bowls, a section entirely dedicated to the event and the consequences of the death of Christ. Chapters 12-14 form a preface to the pouring out of the bowls, mapping out a Christological reading of the whole of the history of salvation: the creation and the fall of humanity (ch.12), the corruption of political and religious authority (ch.13), and a description of the Old Economy as God's former saving initiative, which is also a prefiguring of his definitive intervention in the death of Jesus Christ (ch.14). Once the scene has been thus set, the bowls are poured out to announce the death of Christ as judgment upon all the consequences of the fall described in chapter 12 (chs. 15-16). This theme is then taken further, in detailed descriptions, two negative and one extremely positive, of the same reality: history is judged in the destruction of Babylon (17,1-19,10), all the evil powers are definitively destroyed in the great Armageddon (19,11-20,15), and finally the chosen ones are gathered into the messianic kingdom, the heavenly Jerusalem (21, 1-22,5). As I have already mentioned, a 'woman' appears in a prominent place in the introduction (ch.12), in the description of the negative judgment that is a consequence of the death of Jesus (chs. 17-18) and in the positive consequence of his death, the New Jerusalem (ch. 21). This cannot be mere chance.

As Apocalypse 12 opens, the woman 'clothed with the sun', a 'sign in heaven', is not the only 'sign'. It is important to notice that exactly the same expression is used for the 'great red dragon'. This beast is also called 'a sign in heaven' (see v.3), but this sign is aggressively standing

before the woman who was about to bear a child,
that he might devour her child when she brought
it forth (v.4).

We have here a scene of brilliance and beauty on the one hand, through the use of the image of a woman. It is here that one must be more critical than normal, as there is an understandable tendency to lift 12,1-2 out of context and make an immediate application to Mary. We must take care not to rush into a Mariological interpretation of the figure, as many cultures have the symbol of a woman to represent humanity in its perfection.[75] The two 'signs in heaven' have to be understood in relation to one another, and the waiting dragon is further identified for us in verse 9:

The great dragon was thrown down,
that ancient serpent, who is called
the Devil and Satan,
the deceiver of the whole world.

The author himself is telling us that the dragon represents the serpent from the story of the fall, as it is told in Genesis 3. What we have in 12,1-6 is not about Mary, Israel or the Church; it is a rereading and a retelling of the story of Genesis 3: the woman and the serpent!

If this is the case, what are we to make of the son? The text tells us that as soon as he is brought forth he is 'snatched up to God'. The verb that I have translated as 'snatched' is powerful and almost violent (Greek: *harpazō* — to snatch, to tear away), and although it is often taken as a reference to the ascension of Jesus, this can hardly be the case, given such a verb. I would insist that it must be interpreted in the light of Genesis 3, which forms the background for the whole of the first part of Apocalypse 12. It appears, therefore, that Apocalypse 12,1-6 tells of humanity at its origins, full of promise, full of beauty, but hunted by 'that ancient serpent', and through the fall, losing its state of original perfection and bliss. This is what is being described in the snatching of the child from the woman: she loses her original blessed state. The only difficulty that this interpretation must still handle is the description of the child in supposedly messianic terms in verse 5:

She brought forth a male child,
one who is to rule all the nations
with a rod of iron.

It must be noticed, however, that exactly this description is used for Christians who are prepared to go the way of the Lamb. They are described as regaining their original blessedness in 1,6, where it is one of the characteristics of the 'kings and priests' of the new humanity redeemed by Christ, and it forms part of the promise to the conqueror in the letter to Thyatira (2,21-29, especially vv.26-27). As Corsini has correctly commented, 'Nothing tells us that the ruling over the nations which will be the destiny of the son must be restricted to Jesus and not to the one who has been promised the same prerogative if he has faith in Jesus and gives witness to him'.[76]

'The woman' in 12,1-6 is humanity, fallen from its state of perfection. Notice that the *place* of the woman alters. In verse 1 she is 'in heaven', while in verse 6 we read:

And the woman fled into the desert,
where she has a place prepared by God,
in which to be nourished for one thousand two hundred and sixty days.

Although this still reflects Genesis 3,23-24, the reference to the desert links the woman's situation with a long biblical tradition, which has its beginnings in the Exodus experience. The desert is ambiguous. It was a place where one could meet God, but it was also a place of never-ending wandering, sinfulness and suffering for such great biblical personalities as Abraham, Moses, David, Elijah and Jesus himself. In the midst of all this suffering and wandering, of course, there was always the guiding hand of God in a pillar of fire, and his nourishment in the quail and the manna. This is the background for John's use of 'the desert'. The woman now finds herself in the desert, cared for and nourished by God for three and a half years — another famous biblical period, taken especially from Daniel 9,24-27, used to refer to a period of severe trial. Humanity has fallen from 'heaven' (v.1) to 'the desert', caught in ambiguity and suffering — yet still cared for by the loving, protective hand of God.

Just as humanity has had a change of place from heaven to the desert, so also has the dragon had a change of place. As I have already pointed out, the dragon is also a sign 'in heaven' (v.3), but through the account of the war in heaven between Michael and his angels and the dragon (vv.7-9):

He was thrown down to earth,
and his angels were thrown down with him (v.9).

God has won his victory in Christ (vv.10-12a), but the situation of 'the woman' — humanity — is still at risk, as now humanity and its tempter are *both* caught in the ambiguity of their earthly, historical experience:

Woe to you, O earth and sea,
for the devil has come down to you in great wrath,
because he knows that his time is short! (v.12b).

This leads John, logically, into his second description of an encounter between 'the woman' and the dragon.

From verse 13 through to verse 16 the desert situation is again described. Most scholars see this as a continuation of verse 6, and would see the account of the battle between Michael and the dragon as a clumsy insertion into the original narrative. Some have simply edited it out of Apocalypse 12, in an attempt to rearrange the text in such a way that it makes more sense. We have already seen that the story of the fall of the dragon to the earth is very important, as it matches the fall of the woman from heaven to the desert. It is very important to notice that what is described in verses 13-16 is quite different from verses 1-6. In the earlier passage we saw that the background was Genesis 3 and John was reflecting upon a fallen humanity, caught in ambiguity, pursued by Satan, but protected and nourished by God 'in the desert'. In verses 13-16 there are several clear references to the historical experience of Israel, in the desert again, but this time in the Exodus itself. As Satan pursues the woman, she is given 'the two wings of the great eagle'. This is a clear reference to Exodus 19,4 and Deuteronomy 32,1, where exactly the same image is used to speak of God's protection of Israel through the Exodus. In verse 15 we read of the serpent pouring out water like a river, but the earth opens up and swallows the water — clearly looking back to the whole Red Sea experience of Israel (see Exodus 14,21-31). The two desert experiences of the woman are not the same. John progresses from his first reflection upon the fall of humanity, its ambiguous situation and its being prey to the dragon (vv.1-6) to the concrete historical experience of Israel (vv.13-16). As God had done for humanity at the beginnings, so has he also done for Israel through their Exodus experience.

Nevertheless, that is not the end of the story:

Then the dragon was angry with the woman,
and went off to make war on the rest of her offspring,
on those who keep the commandments of God
and bear testimony to Jesus (v.17ab).

The whole ambiguity of the rest of the history of salvation is now being described as under way. God's loving protection could be seen at the beginnings and again at the Exodus, but the 'rest of her offspring' are still 'in the desert' — caught in the ambiguity of the human condition — and thus chapter 12 ends with the dragon standing on the sand of the sea (v.17c). This positioning of the dragon on the sand, between sea and land, is very significant, as placed there he is ready to enlist the power and authority of corrupt political authority (the beast 'from the sea' described in 13,1-10) and corrupt religious authority (the beast 'from the land' described in 13,11-8) in his efforts to take the woman and her offspring to himself for ever.

Apocalypse 12 leaves us wondering: which direction will humanity take? Will the history of humanity be a history of self-destruction, as it falls victim to the dragon, or will it be a history of salvation? Who will ultimately be the victor? It appears to me that the further use of the image of 'the woman' in chapters 17-18 and then again in chapter 21 shows that the ambiguity of the human condition can be resolved either by a permanent commitment to the beast 'in the desert' (chs.17-18) or by a permanent commitment to the Lamb 'on a high mountain' (ch.21). In summary of the whole of Apocalypse 12, Corsini has written well: 'The woman of ch. 12 is, therefore, a symbol of humanity in its complex and troubled relationship with God'.[77]

As John describes, through powerful imagery, the consequences of the death of Christ, he shows how this 'complex and troubled relationship' can be resolved. In chapter 17 the beast and the woman reappear, but here they are united in a monstrous intimacy. I will report the text in full, as the vivid language speaks for itself.

And he carried me away in the Spirit into the desert, and I saw a woman sitting on a scarlet beast
which was full of blasphemous names,
and it had seven heads and ten horns.
The woman was arrayed in purple and scarlet,
and bedecked with gold and jewels and pearls,
holding in her hand a golden cup full of abominations and the impurities of her fornication;
and on her forehead was written a name of mystery:
'Babylon the great mother of harlots and of earth's abominations' (17,3-5. A.T.)

The 'scarlet beast', which now supports 'the woman', is clearly the dragon from chapter 12. While in chapter 12 'the woman' was used to indicate humanity's precarious situation after the fall, fleeing from

Satan in the ambiguity of the desert, living under the loving protection of a providential God, here that whole situation has been changed. She no longer flees from the dragon: she is mounted upon it, and her permanent place of residence is 'in the desert'. The woman has been used as a symbol to show that humanity can make a decision to go down the way of the beast, to abandon the loving protection of God — but the result is prostitution and ultimate destruction (ch.18).

The final appearance of the woman symbol comes in chapter 21. If John's use of language and imagery was powerful and expressive in his description of the great harlot, it is equally impressive in its sensitivity in chapter 21. As he describes the gathering of the chosen ones, those who from all time have been prepared to listen to the word of Jesus and to give witness to him, he describes the event as a new and heavenly Jerusalem 'prepared as a bride adorned for her husband' (21,2). The visionary is summoned:

'Come, I will show you the Bride, the wife of the Lamb.'
And in Spirit he carried me away to a great, high mountain,
and showed me the holy city Jerusalem coming down out of heaven from God,
having the glory of God,
its radiance like a most rare jewel, like a jasper, clear as crystal (21,9-12).

The dragon has been destroyed, and the intimacy that exists in this final presence of 'the woman' is the precious intimacy of a bride and wife: she is the Bride and the Wife of the Lamb. In this final moment, 'the complex and troubled relationship with God' which was the result of the ambiguous situation of humanity in chapter 12, has been resolved, as 'the woman' has given herself totally in a loving relationship with the Lamb. Humanity's situation has been entirely changed:

Behold, the dwelling of God is with men.
He will dwell with them, and they shall be his people
and God himself will be with them;
he will wipe away every tear from their eyes,
and death shall be no more,
neither shall there be mourning nor crying nor pain any more,
for the former things have
passed away (21,3-4).

The question I posed at the beginning of this chapter must now be answered in the positive: John the Elder deliberately chose the symbol of 'the woman' to develop one of his central arguments:

humanity was originally blessed, but it fell away into the ambiguity of 'the desert', our corrupt yet beautiful, our sinful yet God-filled journey through history. In that situation an all-protecting God never abandons fragile humanity, and he has offered us the possibility of freedom through the consummate act of the death and resurrection of Jesus of Nazareth:

To him who loves us and has freed us from our sins by his blood and made us a kingdom, priests to his God and Father, to him be glory and dominion for ever and ever (1,5-6).

Nevertheless, again through the symbol of 'the woman' we learn that we can commit ourselves to the ways of the beast, and to ultimate destruction — or to the ways of the Lamb, and to the ultimate bliss of intimacy with him.

Throughout the final part of Apocalypse (12,1-22,5) the author has shown that such possibilities have always been a part of the human experience, and as we saw in our brief analysis of 12,13-16, he uses the experience of Israel to indicate where her choices have led her. For our author the great Armageddon is the ultimate consequence of the whole history of collusion between corrupt political and corrupt religious authority, in service of Satan. It has reached its culmination in the death of Jesus, the consummate result of a collusion between Rome (corrupt political authority) and Israel (corrupt religious authority). However, in their apparent victory they are themselves finally defeated. The message of this part of the Apocalypse is that humanity now has a choice: 'At the level of the full realization of the divine salvific plan: 'It has been done!' (see 10,7 ; 16,17; 21,6). From now on the future is firmly committed to the hands of man.'[78] 'Woman' is the symbol used in Apocalypse 12, 17-18 and 21 to make that message clear.

We must be careful not to draw too much from this fact. John has not done anything new in his use of 'the woman' as a symbol for humanity and Israel. I have already mentioned that the use of such symbolism for humanity was widespread in the ancient world,[79] and the Bible regularly uses woman imagery to speak of Israel (see, for example, Isaiah 37,22; 54,1; 62,4; Ezekiel 16,11-63; Hosea 2,2-23; Canticle of Canticles, *passim*). Nevertheless, it remains strikingly important that such a *central Christian message* is carried by 'woman' symbolism. It becomes even more striking when one notices that the Fourth Evangelist carries the use of this symbol further. He also uses the image of a woman in childbirth as a central feature of one of the major sections of the last discourse (see John 16,21-24). It is also the Fourth Evangelist who begins to merge the developing

Marian theology in the early Church with this very important 'woman' symbol. He *never* calls the mother of Jesus — whom he regards as the first and foremost of all believers — by the name of Mary. In the Fourth Gospel Jesus of Nazareth always calls his mother 'Woman' (see John 2,4 and 19,26).

THE GOSPEL OF JOHN [80]

The Fourth Gospel, the fruit of two generations of reflection upon the mystery of Jesus and the result of the internal tensions that the impact of that mystery was bound to create, is extremely rich in so many ways. All I can hope to do here is to indicate rapidly three moments in Johannine teaching on 'woman'.

1. The women in the Gospel story: the Samaritan woman, Mary and Martha and Mary Magdalene.
2. The passage in 16,21-24, where the powerful image of a woman in childbirth is used in an important context dealing with discipleship.
3. The two moments devoted to the mother of Jesus, one at the beginning of the Gospel, in the Cana miracle (2,1-11), and the other at the end, at the foot of the Cross (19,25-27).

1. THE WOMEN IN THE GOSPEL

All of the scenes in which women play a central role are extremely important, and the reader should not think that I have exhausted their significance in the few points I am about to make. It has been said of the Fourth Gospel that it is like a magic pool, where a child can paddle and an elephant can swim. The more one delves, the more one will find. We must content ourselves with some 'first level' considerations, even though we will find that these considerations are already profound and seriously questioning.

The Samaritan Woman: John 4,7-30

I have argued elsewhere that the section of the Fourth Gospel that runs from Cana (2,1-11) to Cana (4,46-54) is a piece of catechesis deliberately devised by the Evangelist to portray a journey of faith.[81] There is a series of episodes telling of various great characters at different stages in a journey of faith: 'the Jews', Nicodemus, John the Baptist, the Samaritan woman, the Samaritan villagers. These episodes are framed by two examples of perfect faith: the mother of Jesus (2,1-11) and the royal official (4,46-54). Within this context the episode of the Samaritan woman is a profound reflection on the possibility of a journey of faith.

There appear to be two different moments in Jesus' encounter with the Samaritan woman. In the first moment he offers the woman 'living water' (vv.7-15), and in the second the woman comes to suspect that Jesus might be the Messiah, as he has told her the secrets of her private life (vv.16-26).

The point of the first discussion is Jesus' offering the woman 'living water'. Jesus reveals himself as one who can dispense eternal life, and he explains this in terms of water:

Whoever drinks *of the water that I shall give him will never thirst:* the water that I shall give him will become in him a spring of water welling up to eternal life (4,14).

The reaction of the woman is a complete misunderstanding of what has been said to her. Notice that the revelation has been made through direct speech, through the actual 'words' of Jesus. She now throws these 'words' back to Jesus, refusing to take any step that may take her outside categories she can understand and control. In verse 14 Jesus spoke of 'living water' and of spring water 'welling up to eternal life'. The woman now replies, using the very same 'words' of Jesus, but unable to go beyond ordinary water and ordinary springs:

Sir, *give me this water that I may not thirst,* nor come here to draw (v.15).

The woman, in this first instance, fails to grasp the opportunity that Jesus has offered her. She is in no way open to his 'words', in strong contrast to the mother of Jesus in the first Cana miracle, who tells the attendants to 'Do whatever he tells you' (2,5) and the royal official in the second Cana miracle, of whom the Evangelist reports: 'The man believed the word that Jesus spoke to him and went his way' (4,50). The Samaritan woman has merely repeated Jesus' words, drawing them back into her world of water and springs that she can drink and visit. At this stage of her journey, she must be judged as having *no faith*.

However, the story of the Samaritan woman does not end there. She is given a further chance. There are two important points made in the second part of her story. (vv.16-26): the revelation of Jesus (vv.16-19.25-26) and the discussion of true cult (vv.20-24). We are concerned here with Jesus' revelation of himself and the woman's reaction to that revelation.

As the woman has not been able to go beyond material water and geographically situated springs, Jesus now questions her about something within her own experience — her marital situation. This is something that she can understand, but this time it is something about which Jesus should have been totally ignorant! Her reaction to Jesus' telling her about her private life is to eventually confess that Jesus is 'a prophet'. This is already a step further along in her journey of faith in Jesus. As yet she has not come to the whole answer, but that there is something more to Jesus' presence and person is becoming clear to her (v.19). After the section on true cult (vv.20-24) the woman comes back to the fact that he has shown her wonderful things (v.25), and so she hesitatingly suggests that he may be the Messiah (v.25).[82] She has come a long way from her simple request for water, but her journey is not yet over. At her hesitant confession that Jesus might be the Messiah (still a category that *she* could understand and control) Jesus replies with the first use in the Gospel of a central and unique Christological title: 'I am he' (Greek *egō eimi*). Unfortunately, many commentators and translators make this final statement of Jesus into an acceptance of the woman's suggestion that he might be the Messiah, by translating: 'I who speak to you am he' (v.26). This is not the case. Over against the woman's suggestions that Jesus might be the fulfilment of *her* hopes and expectations for a prophet and a Messiah, Jesus further reveals himself as someone who far exceeds such hopes. He replies: '*I am* is the one speaking to you' (Greek: *egō eimi, ho lalōn soi*). The journey is now well and truly under way, and her first task is to go to her fellow villagers and announce the coming of Jesus to them, even though, as yet, she is still wondering:

Come, see a man who told me all that I ever did.
Can this be the Christ?

Into her doubt Jesus has revealed the truth — and we can only surmise that the journey would go on in the light of that truth, as she never again appears in the Johannine story.

An important Gospel theme seems to be carried further here. As an example of the possibilities of a journey from no faith in Jesus as the fullness of the revelation of God, the Fourth Evangelist uses a woman, again breaking all convention (see especially vv. 9 and 27). Once more a woman leads the way, as she draws her fellow villagers to come to Jesus, and to eventually arrive at their confession of faith in Jesus:

It is no longer of your words that we believe, for we have heard for ourselves, and we know that this is indeed the Saviour of the world (4,42).

86

Martha and Mary: John 11,17-44

John 11 stands out, along with John 9 (the story of the man born blind), as an extraordinary example of the Fourth Evangelist's literary skill. As the public ministry of Jesus comes to an end (see 12,36) the Evangelist dramatically presents a series of events (and reflections upon those events) that lead, on the one hand, to the death of Jesus (see 11,1-5 and 45-57), and on the other, to the resurrection of Lazarus (see 11,6-44). Of course, the events blend as one comments upon and leads to the other. For our purposes, however, what is remarkable in this chapter is that, apart from Jesus, the only active characters are two women: Martha and Mary.

In the early part of the story Mary 'sat in the house' while Martha went out to meet Jesus (v.20). Mary comes to Jesus only because she is summoned by Martha in verse 29. On meeting Jesus, Mary confesses her faith in Jesus' authority, yet her disappointment because he arrived too late. She uses exactly the same words as her sister, Martha, who also reprimanded Jesus for his late arrival:

Lord, if you had been here, my brother would not have died (v.32: see v.21).

The deep affection that surrounds this encounter (see vv.33-36) is not only a Johannine attempt to portray the human Jesus, but also an effort to show his reaction to a woman's deep trust in him, which as yet has not gone far enough. It is clear in the light of Mary's anointing of Jesus in the very next section of the Gospel (12,1-8) that this very woman (see 11,2) comes to an unconditional gesture of love and faith.[83] However, in chapter 11 we can only speak of an incipient faith, which will bloom into fullness only after God's glory is revealed in the resurrection of Lazarus (see 11,4.40). In fact, as Jesus points out in 12,7 that she is performing the anointing 'for the day of my burial', the Fourth Evangelist also shows that Mary is also aware of the close link that exists between the resurrection of her brother and the death of her Lord. In the anointing there is no hesitation, but bold trust, in the face of the critical reactions of the male disciples, especially Judas (see 12,4-8). In Mary, through chapters 11-12, we see a hesitant journey of faith blossom into a bold conclusion, and again a woman has been chosen by an Evangelist to show the way.

While Mary's journey began with hesitation, in so far as she had to be summoned to go to meet him (11,20.28), Martha's is the exact opposite. She is full of confidence, and for many scholars, comes immediately to a wonderful confession of faith and a total commitment as early as verse 27:

You are the Christ, the Son of God, he who is coming into the world.

I would like to suggest that this is not the case, but that Martha, like Mary, shows openness to Jesus, but only gradually 'journeys' towards a complete faith in him. There appear to be three stages in her gradually deepening encounter with Jesus.

First Stage:

When Martha heard that Jesus was coming, she went out to meet him (v.20). She has no hesitation in expressing faith in the power and authority of Jesus:

Lord if you had been here my brother would not have died. And even now I know that whatever you ask from God, God will give you (vv.21-22).

When she is told that Lazarus will rise, she answers expressing her belief in that fact as well. However, care must be taken here, as the words of Martha show that she is quite prepared to accept the opinion of the Pharisees and of Jesus himself (as opposed to the opinion of the Sadducees) that there will be a final resurrection from the dead:

He will rise again in the resurrection at the last day (vv.23-24).

At this stage there is certainly trust and confidence in Jesus, but it is severely conditioned by categories that *she* can control, and by *her own* expectations.

Second Stage:

In a second moment, she is the recipient of a word of revelation:

I am the resurrection and the life; he who believes in me,
though he die, yet shall he live, and whoever lives
and believes in me shall never die (vv.25-26).

When asked if she believes this, she replies in terms of her famous confession:

Yes, Lord, I believe that you are the Christ, the Son of
God, he who is coming into the world (v.27).

At this stage, in my opinion, she has received a revelation and a promise that transcends all the limitations of culture and history, including all the first-century messianic expectations. However, her reply is to be strictly interpreted precisely in terms of what was being spoken of and written about in first-century Judaism. Even though what she says sounds ever so true to us, we must understand that we are looking back to the words of Martha through two thousand years of Christian faith, where those titles are now taken to apply *only* to Jesus of Nazareth, in the most exalted fashion. Such was not the case when John wrote this passage. It is clear that 'the Christ' and 'the coming one' (Greek: *ho erchomenos*) were well-worn first-century Jewish expressions, but this is also the case for 'son of God'. This is not necessarily a full and correct Johannine confession of faith, and it could well be based on the Jewish reflections upon Psalm 2,7, 2 Samuel 7,14, Hosea 11,1 and many other texts that spoke of the King, the people and the observant Jew as a 'son of God'.[84] It appears to me that this must be the case, in the light of what follows. Martha, like Mary — and also like the Samaritan woman in the second moment of her encounter with Jesus who revealed himself as 'I am he' (see 2, 25-26) — is on the way to a total commitment of faith. However, at this stage she has not yet broken free from her own historical and cultural conditioning, as can be seen from the rest of the chapter.

Third Stage:

Here we can see that my case for a second stage in Martha's journey of faith is correct. After her confession she returns to Mary and announces that Jesus, 'the teacher' (Greek: *ho didaskalos*), is outside asking for her (v.28). This term, 'the teacher', is also found in the Nicodemus episode, where it is clearly an unsatisfactory title for Jesus (see 3,2). However, what is most telling is her objection — some little time later — to Jesus' command that the stone be rolled back. Could anyone who really believed that Jesus was the resurrection and the life, in the full Johannine sense of those terms, and who had made her own total confession of faith in him as such (vv.25-27), later comment:

Lord, by this time there will be an odour, for he has been dead four days (v.39)?

A further indication that she has not yet arrived at full faith can be found in the conditional and the quasi-reprimand of Jesus' words in verse 40:

Did I not tell you that *if you would believe* you would see the glory of God?

The hint is that she has not yet believed, but that a vision of the glory of God, promised at the beginning of the Lazarus story (see 11,4), is still possible. Nevertheless, true faith is still to come!

Thus, the Martha and the Mary encounters with Jesus in John 11 show two women who see Jesus as their only hope, but whose faith initially falls short of the mark. As I have said as I opened this section, it is important to notice that *only women* are used in this chapter, and that the picture is far from negative. In the face of the incredible revelation of Jesus as the resurrection and the life both in word and in deed, they hesitate at the word, as we have seen. Even though the Evangelist tells us nothing of their immediate reaction to the resurrection of Lazarus, the scene at the very beginning of the next chapter (12,1-8) tells us that they are completely swept off their feet by the deeds of Jesus, as their brother is given back to them alive. Their journey, begun hesitantly, ultimately brings them home. The incident with Mary in 12,1-8 shows that through all of their limitations and hesitations, the conditional of verse 40 has been sorted out. There Martha was told:

If you would believe you would see the glory of God.

They have indeed seen the glory of God in the resurrection of their brother (11,4), and thus they have come to faith. In many ways Mary and Martha are models of a movement of faith described by Jesus during the last discourse:

The words that I say to you I do not speak on my own authority; but the Father who dwells in me does his works. Believe me that I am in the Father and the Father in me; or else believe me for the sake of the works themselves (14,10-11).

Mary Magdalene: John 20,1-2,11-18

We have just seen the way in which the Fourth Evangelist uses his great women figures to illustrate a journey of faith. Mary Magdalene makes the same journey, from no faith to complete faith, and her journey is made possible because of her encounter with the risen Lord. In the Fourth Gospel she plays a vitally important role in the story of the risen Jesus. As we have mentioned, this is basically a specially Johannine use of what is fundamental to all the resurrection accounts, where women were the first at the empty tomb, and first to proclaim that Jesus had risen. Again, I can only hope to sketch in the key moments of her journey of faith.[85]

First Stage:

In John 20, 1-2 Mary discovers the empty tomb, and reports to the disciples: 'They have taken the Lord out of the tomb' (v.2). There is not the slightest hint or suggestion that resurrection may have taken place. If the body is not there, then someone has taken it.

The same attitude is again found, after Peter and the Beloved Disciple's race to the tomb (vv.3-10), when Mary Magdalene's story is resumed in verses 11-15. She sees the empty tomb (v.11) and even 'two angels in white, sitting where the body of Jesus had lain'. None of this makes any impression, as she still replies to their questioning the reason for her tears in terms of:

They have taken away my Lord (v.13).

This completely negative stage of Mary's faith experience then reaches its clearest expression when not even the appearance of Jesus himself moves her. He asks the same question as the angels:

Woman, why are you weeping? Whom do you seek? (v.15).

Without the eyes of faith, Mary remains in her darkness and believes that Jesus is the gardener. Thus, she continues her same line of argument:

Sir, if you have carried him away, tell me where you have laid him, and I will take him away (v.15).

There is still no thought of a possible resurrection.

Second Stage:

Jesus calls her by name — 'Mary' (v.16) — and this leads to the recognition of Jesus and a confession in him as 'Rabboni', associated with a desire to cling to him (vv.16-17). This is clearly an attempt to re-establish the same sort of relationship that she had with him before the 'hour' of his being 'lifted up'. Jesus has to inform her that this sort of relationship is now over, and that an entirely new situation will require a more radical faith. Now the God of Jesus is

the God and Father of all the disciples, and Jesus must return there
for the definitive establishment of that situation:

Go to my brethren and say to them,
I am ascending to my Father and your Father,
to my God and your God (v.17).

Now there is a recognition of the risen Jesus, but her attempts to cling
to him show that she has not yet grasped all the implications of the
faith in the risen Lord. However, she has been given a mission, and
her performance of that mission will bring her to the end of her
journey.

Third Stage:

This stage is short and simple. She returns to the disciples, completely
transformed from her original encounter with them in verse 2,
confessing a faith in Jesus that is also completely transformed. At her
first encounter with him in the garden, she used a title to speak to him
as any other man, with respect: 'Sir' (Greek: *kyrie* — see v.15). Now
she states baldly, in a profound confession of faith:

I have seen the Lord (Greek: *ton kurion*, v.18).

The journey of women to faith has come to its fullest expression. It
is remarkable that John has singled out women to show the dynamics
of the life of faith, moving from nothingness, through the temptation
to commit oneself to Jesus according to one's own controllable
categories and hopes, into a total loss of self in his ways. Yet, the
evidence is there, and again we seem to be in close contact with a
principle and a conviction of the earliest Church: the primacy of
women in the order of faith.

2. THE WOMEN WHO GIVES BIRTH TO A CHILD: JOHN 16,21-24

Despite the lengthy and complicated literary history of the last discourse in the Fourth Gospel (13,1-17,26), it appears to me that it
has been placed in the Gospel in its present form by an Evangelist
whose literary skills we have already sensed in the material that we
have examined.[86] Centered upon the powerful message of mutual
love in 15,12-17, the whole discourse can be seen as framed between

13,1-38, which opens with the theme of the perfection of love (vv.1-3) and closes with the themes of love and glory (vv.31-38), and 17,1-26, which opens with the theme of the perfection of Jesus' glorification (vv.1-5) and closes with the themes of love and glory (vv.24-26). Between these extremities, and around the central piece of 15,12-17, the whole discourse can be understood as unfolding in the way indicated below.[87]

THE STRUCTURE OF THE LAST DISCOURSE: John 13, 1-17, 26						
13, 1-38	14, 1-31	15, 1-11	15, 12-17	15, 18. 16,3	16, 4-33	17, 1-26
13, 1: AGAPE: love TELOS: accomplish 'the hour'						17, 1-5 DOXA: glory TELOS: accomplish 'the hour'
	14, 1-5: Departure to a place. 'Let your hearts not be troubled'				16, 4-11: Departure Spirit	
		15, 1-5a Abide in Jesus: the life-giving vine		15, 18-21 Hatred-persecution due to ignorance		
13, 18-20 Fulfil Scripture (v.18) I have chosen (v.18) Word of Jesus: 'I tell you this now' (v.19) Those sent (v.20).	14, 15-24: Disciples to keep the commandments and to love Jesus, leading to being loved by both Jesus and the Father	15, 5b-7: Abide in Jesus (v.5b) Not to abide in Jesus (v.6) Abide in Jesus (v.7)	15, 12-17 Mutual love (vv.12-14) I have chosen you (vv.15-16) Mutual love (v.17)	15, 22-25: Word of Jesus/Sin (v.22) To have Jesus and the Father (v.23) Works of Jesus/Sin (vv.24-25)	16, 21-24 Sorrow leading to joy: the image of the woman in childbirth — sorrow to joy in the disciples	17, 12-19 Fulfil Scripture (v.12) Joy (v.13) Gift of the Word (v.14) Hatred (vv.14-16) Those sent (vv.17-19)
		15, 8-11 Abide in the love of Jesus		15, 26.16, 3: Exclusion-death due to ignorance		
	14, 30-31 Departure Encouragement				16, 31-33 Departure 'Be of good cheer'	
13, 31-38: DOXA: glory AGAPE: love						17, 24-26 DOXA: glory AGAPE: love

As is immediately obvious, the discourse is directed to the disciples of Jesus, and concentrates a great deal of attention on 'the hour' of Jesus' departure. In the Johannine vision of things this 'hour' is regarded as the supreme moment in Jesus' glorification and the ultimate revelation of God's love among men and women (see, for example, 13,1.21-32; 17,1-5). While these magnificent themes dominate the Christology of the discourse, the departure of Jesus creates a problem for the disciples who will be left behind. As can be seen from its structure, the bulk of the discourse is devoted to the last instructions of the departing Jesus to 'his own'.[88]

It is within this overall argument that the passage on the woman in childbirth is found, in 16,21-24. Although in a completely different context, this basic human-female experience was also central to Apocalypse 12,1-6, as we have already seen. Taking 16,4-33 as the literary unit,[89] one finds that this final part of the discourse proper (regarding 13,1-38 as an introduction and 17,1-26 as a summarizing conclusion) is concerned with the pain and sorrow that Jesus' departure will cause. The theme is struck as the section opens (vv.4-6) and it returns as it closes (vv.32-33). A general description of the chapter could be as follows:

verses 4-20: The theme of departure. The pain that will be present among the disciples in the loss of Jesus:

Truly, truly I say to you, you will weep and lament, but the world will rejoice; you will be sorrowful (v.20).

verses 21-24: The joy that comes from suffering, using the image of the woman in childbirth.
verses 25-33: The theme of pain, suffering and trial returns, but now the thrust is one of a newly found peace in the midst of all trials:

In the world you have tribulation, but be of good cheer, I have overcome the world (v.33).

At the center of John's discussion of the transformation of suffering into joy he has used the image of 'woman' to convey a fundamental message on discipleship. This passage has been prepared for in the repetition of the theme of 'now and afterwards' in verses 16 and 19:

A little while, and you will see me no more;
again a little while, and you will see me.

Jesus applies this theme of 'now and afterwards', which is puzzling the disciples (see vv.17-18), as he answers their queries through the image of 'the woman' in verse 21:

During the birth	*After the birth*
A A woman when she is in travail	A When she is delivered of the child
B She has sorrow	
A¹ Because her hour has come.	B She no longer remembers the anguish for joy
	A¹ That a child is born into the world.

The beautiful structure and simple argument based upon the experience of the woman is very clear. The Johannine Jesus next
addresses his disciples' problems by using exactly the same logic in
verse 22:

Now	*Afterwards*
A So you	A *I will see you* again
B have sorrow *now*	B and your hearts will rejoice.

The disciples' experience mirrors the experience of the woman, with
the all-important difference that the woman's joy comes from the
hour of giving birth, while the disciples' joy comes from the renewed
inbreak of the presence of the risen Lord into the life of the disciples.

We must savor the skill of the Evangelist here. He is using one of
the most fundamental of all human experiences, *incarnational* in
every way, to lead disciples of all times to see that sorrow can be
turned into joy through a *receptivity* to the gift of God's Son. Central
to the whole of Johannine thought is a passage that has sometimes
been called a 'mini-Johannine Gospel':

For God so loved the world, that he *gave* his only Son (3,16).

Once that situation of faith and receptivity has taken over the life and
experience of the disciple, then verses 22b-23a will take place. I will
reproduce here my own translation, which attempts to give an
English version of the beautifully balanced original Greek:

A And NO ONE will take your joy *from you*
B In that day
A¹ *me* you will ask for NO THING

The whole argument now returns to the actual situation of the
disciples in the upper room, caught in their doubt and hesitation,
unable to look beyond the anguish of the now. The gift of Jesus only
has to be earnestly sought and it will be given. Providing some unsaid
but implied elements, the argument of verses 23b-24a could run as
follows:

Afterwards	*Now*
A Amen, amen, I say to you, if you will ask anything of the Father in my name	A Hitherto you have asked nothing in my name
B He will give it to you	B (and therefore you have received nothing)
A¹ (because you have asked for it in my name)	A¹ (because you have asked for nothing in my name).

In this situation, the Johannine Jesus can conclude his instruction to the disciples in verse 24b:

Ask, and you will receive, that your joy may be full.

Reflecting on this analysis of John 16, 21-24 within the argument of this book, it appears to me that there are two important features that must be noticed.

(a) The image of a woman giving birth to a child in verse 21 stands behind the whole of the instruction to the disciples, as they are led to see that the true disciple of Jesus is one who is open and receptive to the gift of God, in an attitude of prayerful asking. In both situations (the woman in verse 21 and the disciple in verse 24) the result is perfect joy. In the case of the woman, the patient maternal prepared-ness to accept the anguish of childbirth, in itself the fruit of a prior receptivity, is the key to her joy. In the case of the disciple, he is told that his sorrow can only be overcome by a patient receptivity in prayer. Here we have the powerful use of an exclusively 'woman' experience to eventually communicate a message to Christianity itself. It appears to me that the Johannine use of this image is perfectly coherent with the more narrative use of women characters throughout the whole of the Gospel tradition to convey a message of primacy in the quality of receptivity to God's ways, a primacy in faith. It is also perfectly coherent with the Fourth Gospel's special use of women (the Samaritan, Martha and Mary and Mary Magdalene) to communicate such a message through the example of their par-ticular 'journeys' of faith, as we have seen. Perhaps even more significantly, it is closely linked with the theme of a fragile humanity, challenged to go the way of the Lamb, rather than the way of the Beast, which we traced in our analysis of Apocalypse 12,17-18 and 21. That message is also a call to faith in the salvation that — despite all appearances to the contrary — has already been won for human-kind in the death and resurrection of Jesus of Nazareth.

(b) It remains for us to examine the two pieces of material in the Fourth Gospel that deal with the mother of Jesus: the miracle at Cana (2,1-11) and the scene at the foot of the Cross (19,25-27). As we shall see, one of the features of this material is that the name 'Mary' never appears. Instead she is called 'woman' (see 2,4 and 19,26) — exactly the same term as we find here, in 16,21, and which we found in Apocalypse 12,17-18 and 21. Scholars have also pointed to the link that certainly exists between the use of the term 'hour' in 2,4:

My *hour* has not yet come

and the further use of the same term in 19,27:

And from that *hour* the disciple took her to his own home.

Again, in a context where a woman is used to indicate to the disciples how they should overcome the pain and suffering that separation from Jesus will create, we find a further use of the same term:

She has sorrow, because her *hour* has come.

Although the term 'mother' is not found in 16,21, the whole image is that of motherhood. This is so obvious that it needs no proof. Thus, in both 2,1 and 5, and 19,25 and 27, the term is used, and in 19,27 'the mother of Jesus' becomes 'the mother of the disciple'. The links are too obvious and too important to be accidental. We will find, in our analysis of the material dealing with the mother of Jesus in the Fourth Gospel, that the experience of 'the woman' used in 16,21 to instruct the disciples will be shifted from image to action in the experience of the first of all disciples: 'the woman' — the mother of Jesus.

3. WOMAN! THE MOTHER OF JESUS IN THE FOURTH GOSPEL

The Miracle at Cana: John 2,1-11

I indicated above that the section of the Gospel that runs from 2,1 to 4,54 is deliberately constructed by the Evangelist to teach his readers the nature of authentic faith. All-important in this presentation are the two literary 'frames' around the narrative: the two Cana miracles (2,1-11 and 4,46-54).[90] While insisting that I am not exhausting the message of these two rich passages, we must glance at the unity of structure and message that can easily be seen between the two miracle stories. This parallel is not always recognized, but a careful analysis shows a number of very interesting correspondences.

2,1: 'On the third day there was a marriage at Cana in Galilee.'	4,43.46: 'After two days he departed to Galilee . . . So he came again to Cana in Galilee.'

By referring to 'two days' in the introductory 4,43, John may want the reader to see that even in the case of the second of the two Cana miracles, Jesus comes to Cana in Galilee 'on the third day' (see 2,1). Although this link may be a little speculative, there can be no doubt about the deliberate link set up by the repetition of 'Cana in Galilee', and in the Evangelist's telling his readers that he 'came *again*'. He is obviously looking back to 2,1-11.

A look at the miracle stories themselves shows that the link between the two accounts runs even deeper than an identity of place and perhaps chronology. Breaking all the form-critical rules for 'miracle stories',[91] John constructs *both* stories in a most interesting parallel fashion:

2,1-11:
1. *Problem*: The wine failed (v.3).
2. *Request*: The mother of Jesus said to him, 'They have no wine' (v.3).
3. *Sharp rebuke*: O woman, what have you to do with me? (v.4).
4. *Reaction*: His mother said to the servants, 'Do whatever he *tells* (Greek verb: *legein*) you' (v.5).
5. *Consequence*: A miracle, which leads to the faith of others (disciples) (vv.6-11).

4,46-54:
1. *Problem*: An official whose son was ill (v.46).
2. *Request*: He went down and begged him to come and heal his son (v.47).
3. *Sharp rebuke*: Unless you see signs and wonders you will not believe (v.48).
4. *Reaction*: 'Go, your son will live.' The man believed *the word* (Greek: *logos*) that Jesus spoke to him (v.50).
5. *Consequence*: A miracle, which leads to the faith of others (the household) (vv.51-53).

Both scenes are rounded off with a comment from the Evangelist that again shows that he is attempting to draw his readers' attention to his deliberate statement and restatement of much the same themes through these two Cana miracles:

2,11: This, the first of his signs, Jesus did at Cana in Galilee.

4,54: This was now the second sign which Jesus did when he had come from Judea to Galilee.

These two passages have been constructed with great care, to form what literary critics call an 'inclusion'. This means that they form a sort of 'frame' around the rest of the narrative by stating and restating the same themes, and by using the same sort of literary patterns, so that the reader will see what the *whole section* is ultimately all about. In an inclusion, it is the theme of the 'frame' that determines the overall argument of the whole passage — in our case, the whole section from 2, 1 to 4, 54. What must be seen, therefore, is that Jesus' interlocutors in each case (his mother and the official) *commit themselves to his word*, cost what it may. In both cases we have the background of the Greek term 'logos' (word): 'Do whatever he *tells* you' in 2, 5, where the verb *legein* is used, and 'He believed *the word*; in 4, 50, where the noun *logos* is used. In the midst of a multitude of theological innuendoes that scholars find in these passages (and especially in the first Cana miracle) a most important point is that the mother of Jesus and the official are used as examples of correct faith. They do not need 'signs' to come to faith (see 2, 23-25); they simply trust and commit themselves to *the word* of Jesus.

However, while there is a close parallel between the mother of Jesus and the official, there are two very important points about the faith of the mother of Jesus that place her in a special category.
(a) Within the Johannine narrative structure, she is the *first* person to come to faith. In the Johannine version of things, life is only possible for those who are prepared to place all their faith and trust in what Jesus has come to reveal. This is what is meant by a radical commitment to 'the word of Jesus'. It is not simply that one is called to give intellectual assent to all that he 'says'. One must be prepared to compromise oneself for the whole event of Jesus himself, as the unique once-and-for-all revealing Son of God. In the first Cana miracle the mother of Jesus is presented as the first person in the whole of the Gospel story told by John who is prepared to make such a commitment. Immediately previous to the Cana miracle, in 1, 50-51, Jesus promised what would be seen, if only one would believe:

You shall see greater things than these . . . You will see heaven opened, and the angels of God ascending and descending upon the Son of Man.[92]

This is now fulfilled as Mary takes the risk of trusting in his word — 'Do whatever he tells you' (2,5) — resulting in a miracle, which shows forth the glory of Jesus and leads his disciples into their first moment of belief (see 2,11). Thus, even in this very first appearance of the mother of Jesus, her faith leads to the incipient faith of the disciples. Already at Cana we have the first hint of the theme that will stand at the center of the scene at the Cross, where the mother of Jesus becomes the mother of the disciple.
(b) The Evangelist uses the terms 'mother of Jesus', 'woman', and he links her with 'the hour' of Jesus (see 2,1.3.4.5). These terms point further into the Gospel, into two further passages where they reappear. One we have already considered, in our analysis of John's use of the image of the woman in childbirth to instruct the disciples of Jesus (16,21-24), and the other is the scene at the Cross. There,

through the use of the same terms, the Fourth Evangelist shows that the quality of the faith of the mother of Jesus makes her the 'Mother of the Church', the mother of all disciples.

The Scene at the Cross of Jesus: John 19,25-27

The Johannine passion account is a profoundly theological rewriting of the traditional passion story.[93] Central scenes are the trial before Pilate, where the Kingship of Jesus is proclaimed (see 18, 33-38a; 38b-40; 19,14-15) and enacted (19,1-3), and then the Cross scene, where his Kingship is again proclaimed through the title nailed to the Cross (see 19,19-22) and where he exercises his Kingly role, especially in the central scene of 19,25-27, where he founds his Church.

The main issue of 19,25-27 is clearly ecclesiological. Jesus, 'lifted up' on his Cross (see 3,14; 8,28; 12,32), after the indications of the seamless garment (vv.23-24) that the Church will never be divided, not even in the hands of its enemies, now founds his new 'family'. To do this he chooses two very important 'models': the mother of Jesus, and the beloved disciple. We have already seen that 'mother of Jesus — the woman' has appeared in the Cana miracle as the first person in the Johannine story to come to faith, as she was prepared to commit all to the word of Jesus. Notice how the Evangelist takes up again the terms that he used in that scene: 'mother of Jesus' (vv.25-26) and 'woman' (vv.26-27). She is the model of faith, and she is given as 'mother' to the man whom the Fourth Gospel clearly presents as the model of all disciples. For the Fourth Gospel this unnamed disciple is the disciple whom Jesus loved, the disciple who leant on his breast at the last supper (13,21-26), the disciple who came to faith at the empty tomb, after outrunning the more sluggish Peter (20,3-10).[94] While the mother of Jesus is clearly the first to believe, and thus the model of the believer, the beloved disciple is also used as a model, a model of the disciple of Jesus. Now we can begin to see the implications of this short, beautiful but theologically profound scene. The Church is founded when the first of all believers (the mother of Jesus) and the first of all disciples (the disciple whom Jesus loved) are given one to another. In his death (vv.28-30) Jesus brings to perfection the task that he has been given (see 4,34 and 17,4) and he pours out his Spirit upon the church gathered at his feet (19,30). Little wonder that John picks up yet another term that has run through his whole Gospel, and that has been central to the 'woman' scenes of 2,1-11 and 16,21-24, as he concludes:

And from that *hour* the disciple took her to his own home (19,27).

'The hour', so long expected throughout the Gospel (see 2,4; 7,6-8; 7,30; 8,20; 12,23; 13,1; 17,1), has been brought to its perfection; the Church, the ongoing presence of Jesus among men and women, has been founded.

E. C. Hoskyns, a celebrated English New Testament scholar, who has written a really wonderful commentary on the Fourth Gospel, has written well of this scene, and of this 'hour':

At the time of the Lord's death a new family is brought into being. If the unity of the Church is symbolized by the seamless robe, the peculiar nature of that unity is indicated here. The Church proceeds from the sacrifice of the Son of God, and the union of the Beloved Disciple and the Mother of the Lord prefigures and foreshadows the charity of the Ecclesia of God.[95]

However, there is more to be said. It is important to notice that the relationship established between the mother of Jesus and the beloved disciple is that of 'mother-son'. If John only wished to communicate a message of 'the charity of the Ecclesia of God', then why is there such a powerful insistence upon the term 'mother' within this scene? It appears five times in these few verses. The message may be primarily ecclesiological, but there is also an all-important, and related, word here on Mary. Her relationship to the disciple — then and now — is that of 'mother'. The continual use of the term 'mother of Jesus' to speak of Mary has prepared for this vital scene. The 'mother of Jesus' now becomes the 'mother of the disciple'. If we were to take this into more contemporary theological language — a language that John would never have dreamt of — we have here a fitting conclusion to the whole of the developing New Testament idea of Mary, the mother of Jesus. She can now rightly be called the 'Mother of the Church'. What we have here is the logical conclusion and the full flowering of the early Church's consciousness of the primacy in time and the quality of the faith of Mary of Nazareth.

In this way the Fourth Evangelist has brought to a fitting conclusion a gradually developing understanding of the place and role of woman in the Church, as we find it witnessed to in the best traditions of the New Testament. Through the example of the great women characters (the Samaritan woman, Martha, Mary and Mary Magdalene) he has used women as a vehicle to show the possibility of a journey of faith.[96] Through the image of the patient receptivity of the woman in travail he has taught his disciples that sorrow will be turned into joy, if they will but ask and receive. Finally, through his portrait of the mother of Jesus, he has rounded off his message. The mother of Jesus, even in John, is no distant unattainable figure. She is simply the consummate realization of what was portrayed as possible in all the other women: a quality of a life of faith and receptivity that finds itself in the radical loss of self in a deep and unquestioning trust in the word of Jesus, the revelation of God in the person and message of Jesus of Nazareth.

CONCLUSIONS

Although these reflections are already lengthy, so much more could and should be said on our subject. Any sort of approach to these texts that hoped to avoid all superficiality should really go to even greater lengths. However, a start has been made here, and we will have to content ourselves with our journey so far. Through all of my analysis, it appears to me that Christianity, as it is revealed to us in the major representatives of its earliest writing, has been a major moment in the history of women. The following areas seem central.

1. Woman has been released from the taboo and the myths that have surrounded her in a mystique, yet placed her conveniently on a mysterious side-track. This can already be sensed from the glimpses that our earliest texts gave us of the life of Jesus, and it grew in importance for Paul and for Luke, even though, as we have suggested, Paul obviously had difficulties in the pastoral application of his theological principles. It is also more than probable that Luke's insistence on the importance of women in the life of Jesus (Gospel) and in the story of the early Church (Acts) is an indication that all was not well in his communities. He told the story of Jesus and the Church the way he told it to *correct* situations where women were gradually being pushed back into the roles that they had previously had in the pre-Christian experience of the communities.

2. The greatness of woman appears to emerge from a growing consciousness, especially as we see it reflected in the gospels, that she is first in faith, both in terms of her being the first to come to faith (chronologically) and in the quality of her faith (qualitatively).

3. The infancy stories of Matthew and Luke have shown us that it is not only a 'woman' (Luke), but also 'women' (Matthew) who have played a decisive role in the unfolding of God's salvific plan, precisely because of the primacy of their faith. In all the Gospels, but especially in Luke, once again, this fact is powerfully testified to by the resurrection stories, where women (a woman) are the first to come to the empty tomb, the first to come to Easter faith, and the first to proclaim the Easter message.

4. Particularly in the Apocalypse and in the Fourth Gospel, 'the

woman' becomes a symbol of humanity in all its ambiguity, yet called to greatness because of the death and resurrection of Jesus of Nazareth. In the Apocalypse the possibilities are shown, while in John 'the woman' is used as an example of receptivity upon which all disciples are to model themselves, and from there the final step is taken into the presentation of the mother of Jesus as 'the woman'. Of course, these themes were not invented by the New Testament authors, but the use of this 'woman-language' and symbolism to carry the central message of Christian discipleship leaves no doubt about the place and role of women in the early Church.

5. The use of women in the Fourth Gospel, headed by the mother of Jesus, as 'models' of the possibility of a journey of faith, to which all Christians have been called, shows a clear consciousness of the fact that women are not only the *first* in this area, but they are also *to be followed*. This means that, in the order of faith, women assume the role of leaders.

These are the main conclusions that have come to me over the years, as I have looked at these texts. As I have gradually seen these themes emerge from my analysis, two serious problems have been bothering me more and more. I will simply leave them with you, as I have no immediate and easy solution to them.

(a) What can we do to make it clear to all — the women themselves, as well as the men who dominate the Christian Church — that we have remythologized woman? The study of the sources of our faith indicates that we must repeat in our own age what Jesus of Nazareth and the early Church seem to have done: a demythologization.[97] In the New Testament, woman is clearly first in time and and quality in the order of faith, and thus she assumes a leadership role in man's search for faith. Although many of us have had this experience in our own lives — mothers, wives, close female friends who have led us into our journey of faith — are we conscious enough that when it comes to faith it is regularly women, not men, who lead the way?

(b) Even if we have arrived at that consciousness, given the structure of the Church as we have it today, is it possible for women to assume their role as leaders in the area of faith?

The present ambiguity in the Church's attitude to women is not new. I have already indicated that the pseudo-Pauline literature and some later additions to his authentic letters show that already at the end of the first century a battle was being waged within the Church, against the radical newness that had broken into history in the person and message of Jesus of Nazareth, and that has been faithfully transmitted in the major documents I have attempted to analyze. By the middle of the second century the *Gnostic Gospel according to Thomas* can take the empty tomb stories — so full of the primacy of women in the canonical Gospels — and rewrite them as follows:

Simon Peter said to them [the risen Jesus and his disciples]: Let Mary go out from among us, because women are not worthy of life. Jesus said: See, I shall lead her, so that I will make her male, that she too may become a living spirit, resembling you males. For every woman who makes herself male will enter the kingdom of heaven (Logion 114).[98]

Somewhere, somehow, something has gone terribly wrong! What has become of Jesus' words: 'Whoever does the will of God is my mother, my brother and my sister?' And what of Paul's insistence that 'In Christ there is no male and female?' The battle between the absolutes of culture and history and the radical newness of 'life in Christ' has been apparently lost, but the Lord of history and of his Church will not allow it to remain that way. As Elisabeth Schüssler Fiorenza has so rightly argued: 'Jesus called for a discipleship of equals that still needs to be discovered and realized by women and men today.'[99]

Our post-Conciliar Church still has to suffer the pains of genuine renewal, with all its stops and starts, false moves and one-way streets, but the renewal is with us, and the Spirit that permeates it is leading us, often despite ourselves, into God's future.[100]

May I suggest, in conclusion, that authentic renewal in the Christian Church will come from our women? As we see from the New Testament evidence that we have examined, it is women who have the openness, softness, courage, intuition and staying power that is needed. God made women 'receptive', and that is what gives them their primacy in the Kingdom (see, for example, Mark 9,33-37). A man wants his power and his security — and far too many of us, now as in the past, have found it in the upper echelons of the hierarchical structure of the Christian Churches.

In recent years there have been some valiant attempts to strike out along new paths — and here I would like to mention the prophetic quality of the lives of many Sisters and Religious Congregations over the past twenty years. However, it appears to me that we have arrived at a rather crucial moment. In the face of criticism from all sides, from within the ranks, as well as from outside them, in the face of the loss of many good and talented people who 'just can't take it any more', discouragement and division have crept in.

May I conclude a book that I have written for Christian men and women from all walks of life with a personal note to my women readers? I am well aware that much damage has resulted from woman's presence in the front line in recent years — but that is where you have always been, in the Christian view of things! Please do not let us down now, when at last we males are beginning to see just how much we need you to guide us into a future that only God can determine. This is, ultimately, a journey of faith — and you must once again be prepared to assume the leadership for such a journey.

NOTES

TO THE PREFACE

[1] I have taken this expression from the title given to a whole issue of *Chicago Studies* 19 (1980).

[2] Most recently, and outstandingly, in the hermeneutical and biblical area, by E. S. Fiorenza, *In Memory of Her. A Feminist Reconstruction of Christian Origins.* A word must be said about this important book, which arrived in Australia after I had finished my typescript (but I have attempted to make continual reference to it throughout my notes). Fiorenza, as the subtitle of her book indicates, is asking a vitally important question: 'Were women as well as men the initiators of the Christian movement?' (p.xviii). She, like all scholars asking that question, is faced with the difficult task of first developing a hermeneutical approach and then applying such an approach to the androcentric and patriarchial texts of the early Church. She does it superbly, and I believe that she goes a long way to prove her contention that 'Regardless of how androcentric texts may erase women from historiography, they do not prove the actual absence of women from the center of patriarchal history and biblical revelation' (p.29). She seeks a method to 'transform androcentric historiography into our common history' (p.70). Rosemary R. Ruether, in *Sexism and God-Talk. Towards a Feminist Theology*, p.18, also writes of the need for such an approach: 'To look back to some original base of meaning and truth before corruption is to know that truth is more basic than falsehood ... To find glimmers of this truth in submerged and alternative traditions through history is to assure oneself that one is not mad or duped. Only by finding an alternative historical community and tradition more deeply rooted than those that have become corrupted can one feel sure that in criticizing the dominant tradition one is not just subjectively criticizing the dominant tradition but is, rather, touching a deeper bedrock of authentic Being upon which to ground oneself. One cannot wield the lever of criticism without a place to stand.' See also E. Moltmann-Wendel, *The Women around Jesus. Reflections on Authentic Personhood*, pp.1-12 and M. A. Tolbert, 'Defining the Problem: The Bible and Feminist Hermeneutics', *Semeia* 28 (1984) 113-26.

[3] See Fiorenza, *In Memory of Her*, p.xvi: 'Usually anyone identified with the "feminist cause" is ideologically suspect and professionally discredited. As one of my colleagues remarked about a professor who had written a moderate article on women in the Old Testament: "It is a shame, she may have ruined her scholarly career." '

[4] Three very recent publications have guided me very strongly in my analysis of the New Testament, and in many ways have created my interest in the whole question. I will refer to them in detail through the rest of the book, but they are: G. Dautzenberg, H. Merklein and K. Müller (eds.), *Die Frau im Urchristentum*; E. Corsini, *The Apocalypse. The Perennial Revelation of Jesus Christ*; Y. Simoens, *La gloire d'aimer. Structures stylistiques et interprétatives dans le discours de la Cène*, especially pp. 163-7.

⁵ See, for a useful survey, the work of the Catholic Biblical Association of America's task force report in 'Women and Priestly Ministry: The New Testament Evidence', *The Catholic Biblical Quarterly* 41 (1979) 608-13. See also the fine article of G. Lohfink, 'Weibliche Diakone im Neuen Testament', in *Die Frau im Urchristentum*, pp.320-38.

⁶ This is sometimes a defect found in current literature. See, for example, E. Tetlow, *Women and Ministry in the New Testament*. This is a well-researched and very useful book, but often too much is drawn from subtle historical possibilities.

⁷ See, for example, the excellent review article of R. S. Kraemer, 'Women in the Religions of the Greco-Roman World', *Religious Studies Review* 9 (1983) 127-39. See also the further useful survey of R. Mortley, *Womanhood. The Feminine in Ancient Hellenism, Gnosticism, Christianity and Islam*.

⁸ Most useful is E. and F. Stagg, *Woman in the World of Jesus*, pp.13-100.

⁹ See, on this, D. Goergen, *The Sexual Celibate*, pp.64-72, and the important reflections on the significance of this fact in P. Agudo, 'Intimacy with self versus self-alienation', in A. Polcino (ed.), *Intimacy: Issues of Emotional Living in an Age of Stress for Clergy and Religious*, pp.15-23. See also R. R. Ruether, *Sexism and God-Talk*, pp.93-115.

TO THE TEXT

¹ For a regular review of scholarship in the various areas of women's studies, see *Signs: Journal of Women in Culture and Society*. This journal was first issued in 1975, and has appeared regularly since. Some indication of the theological discussion (only part of the larger discussion) can be found in a large bibliography prepared by Clare B. Fischer in 1974 and added to in 1975 by Clare Fischer and Rochelle Gatlin. These bibliographies were released by the Office of Women's Affairs of the Graduate Theological Union at Berkeley under the title *Woman: A Theological Perspective*. 1984 saw the first number of an important new journal: *The Journal of Feminist Studies in Religion*.

² See, on this, the leading commentaries: G. von Rad, *Genesis. A Commentary*, pp.80-3, and B. Vawter, *On Genesis. A New Reading*, pp.73-6.

³ See again, G. von Rad, *Genesis*, pp.89-93, and B. Vawter, *On Genesis*, pp.79-86.

⁴ On this, see the two opening essays in R. E. Brown, *The Critical Meaning of the Bible*: 'The Human Word of the Almighty God' (pp.1-22) and 'What the Biblical Word Meant and What it Means' (pp.23-44).

⁵ See M. Daly, *Beyond God the Father: Towards a Philosophy of Women's Liberation*; E. S. Fiorenza, *In Memory of Her. A Feminist Theological Reconstruction of Christian Origins*. Sandra Schneiders has made many contributions, especially in the biblical area. See, for example, S. M. Schneiders, 'Women in the Fourth Gospel and the Role of Women in the Contemporary Church', *Biblical Theology Bulletin* 12 (1982) 35-45. I particularly appreciated her sensitive article, 'The Effects of Women's Experience on Their Spirituality', *Spirituality Today* 35 (1983) 100-16. Monika

Hellwig is now a major voice in the American theological scene. See, most recently, her major study of Christology: *Jesus, The Compassion of God. New Perspectives on the Tradition of Christianity.* Maria Boulding, OSB was largely responsible for the important chapter on 'Celibacy' in D. Rees and others. *Consider Your Call. A Theology of Monastic Life Today*, pp.154-88. See also Maria Boulding, *The Coming of God*; Rosemary Radford Ruether, *Sexism and God-Talk. Towards a Feminist Theology*; E. Moltmann-Wendel, *The Women around Jesus. Reflections on Authentic Personhood.* Very indicative of the growing importance of women's contribution to Christian theology is the whole issue of *Chicago Studies* 19 (1980) 111-226, dedicated to the theme 'The Voices of Women' and the whole issue of *National Catholic Reporter* 20 (No. 25: April 13, 1984): 'Women Doing Theology'.

[6] See R. E. Brown *et al., Mary in the New Testament*, pp.241-82: 'Mary in the Literature of the Second Century'. For further developments, see H. Graef, *Mary: A History of Doctrine and Devotion.* For an excellent collection of the apocryphal material, well illustrated and with short introductions to each apocryphal Gospel, see A. Horton, *The Child Jesus.*

[7] See, for example, J. P. Kenny, *The Meaning of Mary for Modern Man*; P. Bearsley, 'Mary the Perfect Disciple: a Paradigm for Mariology', *Theological Studies* 41 (1980) pp.461-504. See also, F. J. Moloney, *Mary: A Gospel Portrait.*

[8] See especially, W. E. Phipps, *The Sexuality of Jesus.* Phipps infers that Jesus had a positive attitude to his own sexuality because of his commendations of marriage and his considerate treatment of women. For a recent ill-founded interpretation of Jesus as the founder of a homosexual sect, see M. Smith, *The Secret Gospel. The Discovery and Interpretation of the Secret Gospel According to Mark.* See the convincing rebuttal of Smith's arguments in R. E. Brown, 'The Relation of "The Secret Gospel of Mark" to the Fourth Gospel', *The Catholic Biblical Quarterly* 36 (1974) 466-85, and in Q. Quesnell, 'The Mar Saba Clementine: A Question of Evidence', *The Catholic Biblical Quarterly* 37 (1975) 48-67.

[9] For surveys of this material, see J. Blank, 'Frauen in den Jesus überlieferungen', pp.9-39; E. and F. Stagg, *Woman in the World of Jesus*, pp.101-60; K. H. Schelkle, *The Spirit and the Bride. Woman in the Bible*, pp.67-90. Most important of all, however, is E. S. Fiorenza, *In Memory of Her*, pp.99-159. Fiorenza would probably be critical of my approach, as she is unhappy with works that limit themselves to 'woman' passages (see, for example, her remarks on pp. 13 and 30). Yet I hope that I am making some sort of contribution to her desire to research 'how much some biblical traditions contain emancipatory elements that have transcended critically their cultural patriarchal contexts and have contributed to the liberation of people, especially of women, although these texts and traditions were embedded in a patriarchal culture and preached by a patriarchal Church' (p.33).

[10] I am presupposing that Mark was the first Gospel to be written, and that both Matthew and Luke used Mark's Gospel as a source. I am well aware that this is often questioned. For a valid recent restatement of the position that I have adopted, see J. Fitzmyer, 'The Priority of Mark and the "Q" Source in Luke', in *To Advance the Gospel. New Testament Studies*, pp.3-40.

[11] For a useful analysis of this material, see E. and F. Stagg, *Woman in the world of Jesus*, pp.126-43.

[12] For detail and further Jewish texts, see H. L. Strack and P. Billerbeck, *Kommentar zum Neuen Testament aus Talmud und Midrasch*, vol. 1, p.480.

[13] V. Taylor, *The Gospel According to St. Mark*, p.296. See, for the same opinion, the important commentaries of M. J. Lagrange, *Evangile selon Saint Marc*, p.139; R. Pesch, *Das Markusevangelium*, vol. 1, p.311; H. Anderson, *The Gospel of Mark*, p.156.

[14] R. E. Brown, *The Birth of the Messiah*, p.123. See further, J. Jeremias, *Jerusalem in the Time of Jesus. An Investigation into Economic and Social Conditions during the New Testament Period*, pp.365-68.

[15] The RSV has *cumi*, which would be the proper Aramaic feminine form. However, the best reading should retain the more difficult masculine *cum*. On this, see B. M. Metzger, *A Textual Commentary on the Greek New Testament*, p.87.

[16] H. Anderson, *Mark*, pp. 191-2.

[17] I came to these conclusions from my own reading of the text, *in spite* of all of the commentaries that I had consulted. Since writing my own reflections, I have now read —with much pleasure (and not a little pride)—the following reflection of Elisabeth Fiorenza, *In Memory of Her*, p.124, connecting the account of the woman with the flow of blood and the daughter of Jairus: 'This story [the woman with the flow of blood] was probably interlinked with the story of the daughter of Jairus, one of the rulers of the synagogue, not only because of the catchword *twelve* but also because it proclaims the same understanding of wholeness and holiness. Jesus touches the dead girl and thus becomes 'unclean' (cf. Num 19:11-13). Yet the power of the *hasileia* does not rest in holiness and cultic purity. The girl gets up and walks, she rises to womanhood (Jewish girls became marriageable at twelve). The young woman who begins to menstruate, like the older woman who experiences menstruation as a pathological condition, are both "given" new life. The life-creating powers of women manifested in "the flow of blood" are neither "bad" nor cut off in death but are "restored" so that women can "go and live in *shalom*", in the eschatological well-being and happiness of God.' See further, R. C. Wahlberg, *Jesus According to a Woman*, pp.31-41.

[18] On these vocation stories, and their implications for an understanding of Mark's Gospel, see F. J. Moloney, 'The Vocation of the Disciples in the Gospel of Mark', *Salesianum* 43 (1981) 487-516 and *idem, Disciples and Prophets. A Biblical Model for the Religious Life*, pp.135-40.

[19] See, for a full discussion of the evidence, B. M. Metzger, *A Textual Commentary*, pp.219-22. For a good analysis of the passage, as well as the usual commentaries, see J. Blank, 'Frauen in den Jesus überlieferungen', pp.82-8.

[20] D. Rees and others, *Consider Your Call*, p.169.

[21] See J. Blank, 'Frauen in den Jesus überlieferungen', p.33; E. Schweizer, *The Good News according to Matthew*, pp.410-11; J. Jeremias, *The Parables of Jesus*, pp.80-1.

[22] See, on this, E. Schweizer, *Matthew*, pp.465-6; J. Jeremias, *The Parables of Jesus*, pp.51-3. See especially pp.171-5, for Jeremias' reconstruction of the *situation in the life of Jesus* that may have given birth to the parable.

²³ See especially, E. Corsini, *The Apocalypse*, pp.341-4.

²⁴ For a good comparative study, see J. Blank, 'Frauen in den Jesus überlieferungen', pp.22-8. See, however, the more reflective and moving commentary of E. Moltmann-Wendel, *The Women around Jesus*, pp. 93-104, especially her important remarks on 'corporeity' and touching, on pp.101-4.

²⁵ See, on this scene, F. J. Moloney, *The Johannine Son of Man*, pp.160-73. See also E. Moltmann-Wendel, *The Women around Jesus*, pp.51-8.

²⁶ The magisterial study of the *events* surrounding the empty tomb is still that of H. von Campenhausen, 'The Events of Easter and the Empty Tomb', in *Tradition and Life in the Church. Essays and Lectures in Church History*, pp. 42-89. For an excellent synthesis of current discussion, see R. E. Brown, *The Virgin Birth and the Bodily Resurrection of Jesus*, pp.69-133. For a perceptive study of Mark's use of women in his theology of discipleship, see E. S. Fiorenza, *In Memory of Her*, pp.316-23. See also W. Munro, 'Women Disciples in Mark?' *The Catholic Biblical Quarterly* 44 (1982) pp.225-41 and E. S. Malbon, 'Fallible followers: Women and men in the Gospel of Mark', *Semeia* 28 (1983) pp. 29-48. A most useful study of each Evangelist's presentation of the events at the empty tomb can be found in E. L. Bode, *The First Easter Morning. The Gospel Accounts of the Women's Visit to the Tomb of Jesus*.

²⁷ While this is generally admitted for Matthew, some scholars have long argued that the Lucan passion story comes from a Lucan source that had no contact with Mark (the so-called 'proto-Luke'). For this case, see, most recently, V. Taylor, *The Passion Narrative of St Luke*. For the position I have adopted, see Fitzmyer's article referred to in note 10 above.

²⁸ See the discussion of E. and F. Stagg, *Woman in the World of Jesus*, pp.144-60. Also excellent, and theologically perceptive, is H. Ritt, 'Die Frauen und die Osterbotschaft. Synopse der Grabesgeschichten (Mk 16, 1-8; Mt 27, 62-28,15; Lk 24, 1-12; Joh 20,1-18)', in G. Dautzenberg *et al.*, *Die Frau im Urchristentum*, pp. 117-33.

²⁹ See, for a brief discussion of this issue, F. J. Moloney, 'Faith in the Risen Jesus', *Salesianum* 43 (1981) pp.305-16. See, especially on the origins of 'the third day' language, H. von Campenhausen, 'The Events of Easter and the Empty Tomb', esp. pp.77-87.

³⁰ Many of the commentators claim that this 'woman' material plays no part in Mark's overall theological argument, and therefore has very good claims to authenticity. Mark has used it because it has come to him this way in his traditions. See, for example, V. Taylor, *The Gospel according to St. Mark*, pp.178, 347. E. S. Fiorenza, *In Memory of Her*, pp. 316-23, has shown that *despite* the powerful 'patriarchilization' of the late first-century Church, the Gospel of Mark could still use women as 'paradigms of true discipleship'. Again, I would suggest that this is closely linked to the historical development of the Gospel 'form'. A part of this development was a deeply-felt loyalty to the authentic memory of Jesus. See also E. Moltmann-Wendel, *The Women around Jesus*, pp.107-17.

³¹ The theme of 'reversal' runs through the whole of the Old Testament. One need mention only some of the more outstanding examples: the choice of David (1 Samuel 16,1-13), the vocation of some of the prophets (Jeremiah, see Jeremiah 1,6-8; and Amos, see Amos 7,14-15), the message to abandon the criteria of military and political

power (Isaiah 7 and Daniel 7, for example). The great women characters in the Old Testament can be seen in the same light, especially Ruth and Esther. The life and teaching of Jesus seem to be strongly marked by this idea (see, for example, Mark 8,34-9,1; 9,35-37; 10,42-45).

[32] For a good survey, see E. and F. Stagg, *Woman in the World of Jesus* pp.15-32. See also M. Greenberg, 'Crimes and Punishments', in *The Interpreter's Dictionary of the Bible*, vol. 1, pp.739-40, on sexual crimes. The whole article runs from p.733 to p.744.

[33] For a full discussion, see F. J. Moloney, 'Matthew 19,3-13 and Celibacy. A Form Critical and Redactional Critical Study', *Journal for the Study of the New Testament* 2 (1979) pp.42-60. See also the further bibliography listed there. See further, the most interesting more general article (which also touches these questions): J. C. Anderson, 'Matthew: Gender and Reading', *Semeia* 28 (1983) pp.3-27.

[34] This message runs right across the New Testament (see Mark 10,1-12; Matthew 5,31-32; 19,3-12; Luke 16,18; 1 Corinthians 7,10-16). Even the 'exception clauses' found only in Matthew (Matthew 5,32 and 19,9) are to be explained as the necessity to allow an illegitimate marriage union (probably contracted while the couple were still pagans) to be dissolved upon entry into the Matthean community. See, for a full study of these passages, F. J. Moloney, 'Matthew 19,3-12 and Celibacy', pp.43-9. A due recognition of this is *vital* for a well-founded and healthy renewal of our 'discipleship of equals' (Fiorenza). While I can understand some of the anger, it pains me to read the half-truths published by Rosemary Ruether, *Sexism and God-Talk*, pp. 260-1: 'The Christian Church teaches that birth is shameful, that from the sexual libido the corruption of the human race is passed on from generation to generation. Only through the second birth of baptism, administered by the male clergy, is the filth of mother's birth remedied and the offspring of the woman's womb made fit to be a child of God . . . She must obediently accept the effects of these holy male acts upon her body, must not seek to control their effects, must not become a conscious decision maker about the destiny of her own body'. As a *male*, deeply committed to 'the Christian Church', I object strongly to her continual use of the present tense in this emotional passage. Whatever woman's experiences may have been, and perhaps still are in some places and under certain unchristian 'Christian' Churches, we are on a journey *together*. It is the *only way* to go, even though the light at the end of the tunnel may only be a faint glimmer.

[35] D. L. Sayers, 'The Human-not-quite-Human', in *Unpopular Opinions*, pp.121-2, as quoted in D. Rees and others, *Consider Your Call*, p.169. As I have reflected upon Jesus' marvellous way with woman, I also read a passage that struck me very profoundly, and that led me to ask a further question. I will simply leave my reflection with you. I started with a reading of Maggie Ross, *The Fire of Your Life. A Solitude Shared*, pp.72-3: 'Something happened at Mass one day that summoned up a little of this interplay of forces at work in the living-out of chastity. I was watching a priest celebrate the Eucharist at fairly close quarters. He celebrated with such an unconscious beauty, with such deftness and sureness, tenderness and strength that the thought — not a fantasy or temptation or anything of that nature — just the words crossed my mind, as naturally and ordinarily as any other reflection: "I wonder if he makes love like that".' Maggie Ross was speaking out of the Anglican tradition, where this was a perfectly legitimate — but O so profound — question. My reflection went that one step further: if such had been the case, with what great sureness, tenderness and strength would Jesus of Nazareth have made love! To repeat an expression from Maria Boulding that I quoted earlier: 'Not only had he no sin, but he must have

completely accepted and integrated his own sexuality. Only a man who has done so
. . . can relate properly to women' (*Consider Your Call*, p.169). See also the interesting
article of E. Moltmann-Wendel, 'Motherhood or Friendship', in H. Kung and J.
Moltmann (eds.) *Mary in the Churches*, pp.17-22.

[36] For a general survey, see G. H. Tavard, *Woman in Christian Tradition*, pp.27-35;
K. H. Schelkle, *The Spirit and the Bride*, pp.157-65; F. X. Cleary, 'Woman in the New
Testament: St. Paul and the Early Pauline Churches', *Biblical Theology Bulletin* 10
(1980) pp.78-82; G. Dautzenberg, 'Zur Stellung der Frauen in den paulinischen
Gemeinden', in *Die Frau im Urchristentum*, pp.182-224; E. and F. Stagg, *Woman in
the World of Jesus*, pp.162-86.

[37] See, for example, W. O. Walker, '1 Cor. 11,2-16 and Paul's Views regarding
Women', *Journal for Biblical Literature* 97 (1978) pp.435-6; G. W. Trompf, 'On
Attitudes toward Women in Paul and Paulinist Literature', *The Catholic Biblical
Quarterly* 42 (1980) pp.196-215.

[38] See, on this, the well-considered and careful commentary of C. K. Barrett, *The
First Epistle to the Corinthians*, pp.329-33. See further, F. X. Cleary, 'Woman in the
New Testament', pp.81-2, and J. Murphy-O'Connor, 1 Corinthians. See the good
survey in A. Feuillet, 'La dignité et la rôle de la femme d'après quelques textes
pauliniennes', *New Testament Studies* 21 (1974-75) pp.162-170. The whole article
runs from p.157 to p.191. Most recently there has been an attempt to explain away the
difficulty. See N. M. Flanagan and E. H. Snyder, 'Did Paul put down Women in 1 Cor.
14,34-36?' *Biblical Theology Bulletin* 11 (1981) pp.10-12.

[39] I will refer only to Murphy-O'Connor's contribution. Further bibliography and
indications of the ongoing discussion can be found in his footnotes. See J. Murphy-
O'Connor, 'The Non-Pauline Character of 1 Corinthians 11,2-16', *Journal for
Biblical Literature* 95 (1976) pp.615-21; *idem*, 'Sex and Logic in I Corinthians
11,2-16', *The Catholic Biblical Quarterly* 42 (1980) pp.482-500; *idem*, *I Corinthians*, pp.104-9.

[40] For what follows, see F. J. Moloney, *A Life of Promise: Poverty, Chastity,
Obedience*, pp.34-8. For a fine analysis of Galatians 3,28, see E. S. Fiorenza, *In
Memory of Her*, pp.205-18. For her different opinion of 1 Corinthians 11,2-16 and
14,33b-36, see pp.226-33, where she claims that both texts are originally Pauline, but
that they have to be 'understood in the context of Paul's argument against orgiastic
behavior in the worship of the community' (p.233). I would like to show that there is
sufficient *internal* cohesion in Paul's understanding of the role of woman (especially
within the overall context of his concept of Christian life being life 'in Christ') to make
sense out of these texts without reaching for a series of *possible* contacts with the
orgiastic practices of women in the Isis and similar cults.

[41] For some of them, see F. J. Moloney, *Disciples and Prophets. A Biblical Model for
the Religious Life*, pp.87-9, and especially, J. Murphy-O'Connor, *Becoming Human
Together. The Pastoral Anthropology of St. Paul*.

[42] See, on this, G. W. Trompf, 'On Attitudes to Women', pp.205-15. Although I
disagree with Trompf on 1 Corinthians 11,2-16, his indications of the tendencies of
the later 'paulinist' literature are most helpful. See also the excellent article (although I
would again differ with the interpretation of 1 Corinthians 11,2-16) of W. O. Walker,
'The "Theology of Woman's Place" and the "Paulinist" Tradition', *Semeia* 28 (1983)
pp.101-12. E. S. Fiorenza, *In Memory of Her*, pp.218-36, would claim that Paul

himself was forced to modify Galatians 3,28 in the light of certain pastoral situations. For her most valuable study of the post-Pauline developments, see pp.245-315.

[43] Although strange to us, the practice of placing a document under the authorship of a major character from the past was a commonly accepted way to give authority to such documents. This does not in any way touch their rightful place within the canon of the New Testament, but it must be kept in mind when one is tracing the developing lines of Christian thought into the end of the first century and the beginnings of the second. On this, see H. Koester, *Introduction to the New Testament*, vol. 2, p.305, and the further bibliography given on p.2.

[44] J. Murphy-O'Connor, 'Sex and Logic', p.498. See also *idem, 1 Corinthians*, pp.104-9.

[45] See R. E. Brown, *The Epistles of John*, pp.47-115.

[46] My claim here is given powerful support by E. S. Fiorenza, *In Memory of Her*, pp.198-9 and pp.208-18. She shows, convincingly, that Galatians 3,28 was not invented by Paul, but was a Pauline continuation of an accepted early Christian idea and practice. As she herself explains: 'Gal 3,28 . . . is not a Pauline "peak formulation" or a theological breakthrough achieved by Paul that is outnumbered by the subordination passages. Gal 3,28 is a key expression, not of Pauline theology but of the theological self-understanding which had far-reaching historical impact' (p.199). Where did this 'theological self-understanding' have its origins? I would suggest that it began in Jesus' own attitude to women, and in his teaching—some of which we have already attempted to analyze.

[47] See, for a short analysis, E. M. Tetlow, *Women and Ministry*, pp.98-101. For a more redactional approach, stressing that there is a uniquely Matthean use of the material, see J. Blank, 'Frauen in den Jesusüberlieferungen', pp.29-39.

[48] For much of what follows, and for detailed discussions of contemporary scholarship, with full bibliographies, see R. E. Brown, *The Birth of the Messiah*, pp.71-4. Full details are also given there for the positions of Jerome and Luther.

[49] For an extraordinary and positive interpretation of the Judah and Tamar episode (an apparent interruption to the flow of the Joseph story), see R. Alter, *The Art of Biblical Narrative*, pp.3-22, especially pp.4-11.

[50] In Matthew 20,20-23, the Evangelist does not allow the sons of Zebedee to ask that they be allowed to sit at the right and at the left of Jesus when he comes to glory, as they do in Mark (see Mark 10,35-40). Matthew has their mother ask for such a privilege (Matthew 20,20). This is clearly a Matthean insertion to maintain the dignity and integrity of James and John, and has nothing to do with Matthew's theology of women. See J. Blank, 'Frauen in den Jesusüberlieferungen', p.29.

[51] See, on this, J. Blank, pp.29-31.

[52] For an excellent up-to-date survey of the theology of Matthew's Gospel, see E. A. Laverdiere and W. G. Thompson, 'New Testament Communities in Transition: A Study of Matthew and Luke', *Theological Studies* 37 (1976) pp.567-97. On Matthew, see pp.571-82. See also D. Senior, *What are they saying about Matthew?* and J. P. Meier, *The Vision of Matthew*.

[53] For a short analysis and evaluation of these two *contrasting* narratives, see F. J. Moloney, 'The Infancy Narratives. Another View of Raymond Brown's "The Birth of the Messiah" ', *The Clergy Review* 64 (1979) pp.161-6.

[54] Once again, see R. E. Brown, *The Birth of the Messiah*, pp.256-329, 412-31, for a full development of these two themes. My analysis depends heavily upon his.

[55] The Lucan references in parenthesis show where this annunciation pattern is fulfilled in Luke 1,26-38.

[56] Unfortunately, the translation 'full of Grace' has sometimes been used as a biblical proof for the doctrine of the Immaculate Conception. The argument runs that when the angel came, she was already 'full of Grace' because of the remarkable privilege of being conceived without original sin. Luke shows no knowledge of this doctrine, which it took the Church nearly nineteen hundred years to decide upon. His use of the passive verb here excludes any such interpretation.

[57] See, on this, B. Byrne, *'Sons of God — Seed of Abraham'. A Study of the Sonship of God of all Christians in Paul against the Jewish Background*, pp.9-78.

[58] See A. Horton, *The Child Jesus*, pp.36-75 for a good collection of these legends. There are also some excellent reproductions of the artistic representations of such legends that have reflected, over the centuries, their importance in popular piety.

[59] See, for somewhat less enthusiastic but still positive evaluation of these texts, R. Mahoney, 'Die Mutter Jesu im Neuen Testament', in G. Dautzenberg *et al.*, *Die Frau im Urchristentum*, pp.103-10. See also the critical and ecumenical approach of J. L. McKenzie, 'The Mother of Jesus in the New Testament', in H. Küng and J. Moltmann (eds.), *Mary in the Churches*, pp.3-11. I have serious objections to McKenzie's thesis. Some of his caustic remarks are simply *not true*: 'Biblical studies about Mary, like Mariology as a whole, have come to a nearly complete halt since Vatican II' (pp.3,10). A rapid glance at M. O'Carroll, *Theotokos. A Theological Encyclopedia of the Blessed Virgin Mary*, along with the bibliographies attached to the articles in the encyclopedia, would be enough to disprove such a statement. However, what concerns me most — from such a significant scholar as J. L. McKenzie — is his rapid conclusion that the scant material in the New Testament on Mary indicates that 'Faith in the Mary of traditional Christian devotion is faith in something which is not true' (p.9). There are many difficulties, and even 'near heresies' in some popular devotions, but I hope to have indicated that a solid traditional devotion to Mary can be firmly based on gospel traditions. Our study of the Fourth Gospel will add even further elements. Rosemary Ruether, *Sexism and God-Talk*, pp.139-58, does see the value of the Lucan portrait of Mary, and of women in general. She then uses it as a symbol for a possible paradigm for a Church 'identified with the cause of the oppressed', and is highly critical of 'the monopolization of the Church by the social establishment' (p.157). While a great deal of what she claims is true, her somewhat myopic fascination with this issue leaves other possibilities unexamined. There is more to New Testament Mariology than either McKenzie or Ruether allows.

[60] See, for an analysis, E. M. Tetlow, *Women and Ministry*, pp.101-9. She also looks at Acts, Luke's second volume. The same themes emerge. See now, on the whole question of women in the early Christian mission, E. S. Fiorenza, *In Memory of Her*, pp.160-204. Her approach is somewhat different to that of Tetlow. While her results are extremely positive, her method is more realistic. Given the nature of the sources

(Acts and Paul), Fiorenza argues that 'women's actual contribution to the early Christian missionary movement . . . must be rescued through historical imagination as well as in and through a reconstruction of this movement which fills out and contextualizes the fragmentary information still availabe to us' (p.167).

[61] See especially, J. Blank, 'Frauen in den Jesusüberlieferungen', pp.39-68. A further helpful article, situating the discussion within the context of contemporary Lucan studies is E. H. Maly, 'Women and the Gospel of Luke', *Biblical Theology Bulletin* 10 (1980) pp.99-104. See the perceptive evaluation of the presence of women as important members of the ever-growing group called 'disciples' in the Lucan presentation of Jesus' ministry, at the supper and into the early Church in Q. Quesnell, 'The Women at Luke's Supper' in R. J. Cassidy and P. J. Scharper (eds.), *Political Issues in Luke-Acts*, pp.59-79.

[62] It is widely admitted that this episode, although it may have its origins in the life of Jesus, has been composed in its present form by Luke. Its setting (see v.34), the parable (vv.41-43) and the polemic (vv.44-47) are very Lucan. On this, see the good summary of J. Blank, 'Frauen in den Jesusüberlieferungen', pp.42-4. Its Lucan character again shows the importance of women to this Evangelist and to his communities.

[63] See, on this, I. H. Marshall, *Luke: Historian and Theologian*, pp.138-40; J. Blank, 'Frauen in den Jesusüberlieferungen', pp.44-8.

[64] See G. B. Caird, *St Luke*, p.115.

[65] See above, pp.20-22.

[66] For a good survey of this widespread attitude to 'Martha', see E. Moltmann-Wendel, *The Women around Jesus*, pp.15-22. For a *very different* idea, having its origins in John II and then reaching a peak in the Middle Ages, see pp.28-48. There Martha is seen as the wise virgin and the conqueror of the dragon.

[67] See G. B. Caird, *St Luke*, p.148.

[68] For a summary of these discussions, see I. H. Marshall, *The Gospel of Luke. A Commentary on the Greek Text*, pp.556-7.

[69] G. B. Caird, *St. Luke*, p.171. See also, E. S. Fiorenza, *In Memory of Her*.

[70] For an analysis of these passages, see J. Blank, 'Frauen in den Jesusüberlieferungen', pp.63-8.

[71] E. H. Maly, 'Women and the Gospel of Luke', p.104.

[72] For a comprehensive survey and a critical evaluation of the suggestions that have been made over the centuries, see C. Brütsch, *La Clarté de l'Apocalypse*, pp.199-203.

[73] Very few scholars have posed this question seriously. Even those who have do not do justice to the internal logic of these final chapters on the seven bowls (12,1-22,5), a section marked by the threefold use of the 'woman' symbol. See, for example, T. Holtz, *Die Christologie der Apokalypse des Johannes*, pp.102-8, and J. M. Court, *Myth and History in the Book of Revelation*, pp.111-14.

⁷⁴ For this interpretation I have been greatly influenced by the work of E. Corsini, *The Apocalypse. The Perennial Revelation of Jesus Christ*, pp.211-25. I would also like to refer the reader to a little book that uses Apocalypse 12 to construct a theology of hope and to exhort all to go on 'bearing life' in the face of a possible nuclear end to history. The author has a different understanding of Apocalypse 12 from the one that follows, but her moving plea for hope and trust is close to what I believe the author is saying. See D. Priestley, *Bringing Forth in Hope. Being Creative in a Nuclear Age*.

⁷⁵ For an excellent survey of the widespread use of this symbol in the ancient near-eastern world, see G. R. Beasley *The Book of Revelation*, pp.192-7.

⁷⁶ E. Corsini, *The Apocalypse*, p.215.

⁷⁷ p.224.

⁷⁸ p.423.

⁷⁹ See above, note 75.

⁸⁰ What follows will come, largely, from my own familiarity with the Fourth Gospel and the literature on it. I will not document every argument, and some of it will appear novel. There is a great deal of literature on this subject. Any interested reader might consult the following specialized works, as well as the great commentaries of Bultmann, Barrett, Brown, Schnackenburg, Lindars and Haenchen. J. Alfaro, 'The Mariology of the Fourth Gospel. Mary and the Struggles for Liberation', *Biblical Theology Bulletin* 10 (1980) 3-16; R. E. Brown, 'Roles of Women in the Fourth Gospel', *Theological Studies* 36 (1975) pp.688-99 (this article has been reprinted in Brown's *The Community of the Beloved Disciple*, pp.183-98); A. Feuillet, 'The Hour of Jesus and the Sign of Cana', in *Johannine Studies*, pp.17-37; S. M. Schneiders, 'Women in the Fourth Gospel and the Role of Women in the Contemporary Church', *Biblical Theology Bulletin* 12 (1982) pp.35-45; E. S. Fiorenza, *In Memory of Her*, pp.323-43. Again Fiorenza does well to show that the Johannine use of women characters is closely related to the Evangelist's attempt to find 'paradigms of true discipleship'. While not wishing to minimalize the skills of the Fourth Evangelist as he uses his women characters as 'symbols', I would still claim that the place of women in John's portrait of a true disciple has its roots in the pre-Easter experience of Jesus.

⁸¹ F. J. Moloney, 'From Cana to Cana (Jn 2,1-4,54) and the Fourth Evangelist's Concept of Correct (and Incorrect) Faith', *Salesianum* 40 (1978) pp.817-43. It is also reproduced in E. A. Livingstone (ed.), *Studia Biblica. II Papers on the Gospels. Sixth International Congress on Biblical Studies. Oxford 3-7 April 1978*, pp.185-213.

⁸² It is often suggested that the Samaritan idea of the Messiah, or the *Ta'eb*, is reflected here. He was expected, among other things, to be a prophetic revealer. This appears to be based upon Deuteronomy 18,18 and is reflected in the 3rd-4th century Samaritan document, the *Memar Markah* IV,12. See R. Schnackenburg, *The Gospel According to St John*, vol. 1, pp.440-1, and R. E. Brown, *The Gospel according to John*, vol.1, pp.170-3, for more detail and further bibliography.

⁸³ On this difficult passage, see my detailed analysis in F. J. Moloney, *The Johannine Son of Man*, pp.168-71.

[84] See F. J. Moloney, 'The Johannine Son of God', *Salesianum* 38 (1976) pp.79-80. The article runs from p.71 to p.86. For a fuller and very clear analysis of the Jewish background for this notion, see B. J. Byrne, '*Son of God — Seed of Abraham*', pp.9-78.

[85] See, for a fuller analysis of this material, F. J. Moloney, 'John 20: A Journey Completed', *The Australasian Catholic Record* 59 (1982) pp.417-32. See also the valuable reflections on the biblical and post-biblical portraits of Mary Magdalene in E. Moltmann-Wendel, *The Women around Jesus*, pp.61-90.

[86] This case has now been convincingly argued by Y. Simoens *La gloire d'aimer. Structures stylistiques et interprétatives dans le Discours de la Cène.* All the necessary references to the whole discussion can be found in Simoen's notes. For a recent very different view, see F. F. Segovia, *Love Relationships in the Johannine Tradition. Agapē/Agapan in I John and the Fourth Gospel*, pp.81-131. In this doctoral thesis and in a number of previous and subsequent articles, Segovia has developed a method of recovering the original setting and meaning of the various component parts of the discourse, and only when he has done that work does he attempt to understand why the Evangelist used it in its present context.

[87] This structure is based upon the analysis of Y. Simoens, *La gloire d'aimer*, pp.52-80. For his own structure, which I have slightly reworked, see p.77.

[88] See, on this, F. J. Moloney, 'John 17: The Prayer of Jesus' Hour', *The Clergy Review* 67 (1982) pp.79-83.

[89] For a detailed analysis of this case, see Y. Simoens, *La gloire d'aimer*, pp.151-8.

[90] See above, pp.84-85 and note 81.

[91] See, for an excellent summary of these 'rules' and the various histories of religious parallels that have helped the form critics to establish them, W. Barclay, *The Gospels and Acts*, vol. 1, pp.33-41. All necessary references to the founding figures of this method (Dibelius, Schmidt and Bultmann) can be found in Barclay's notes.

[92] See, on this passage, F. J. Moloney, *The Johannine Son of Man*, pp.23-41.

[93] For some indications and further bibliography, see F. J. Moloney, *The Johannine Son of Man*, pp.202-7.

[94] For further reflections on this 'race', see F. J. Moloney, 'John 20: A Journey Completed', pp.424-7.

[95] E. C. Hoskyns and F. N. Davey (ed.), *The Fourth Gospel*, p.530.

[96] In a fine reflection on evil and conversion, Rosemary Ruether, *Sexism and God-Talk*, pp.183-92, picks up the theme of 'journey', but has not appreciated the important Johannine background for this theme.

[97] For a fundamental rethinking of this whole issue, see the enormously important work — whatever its limitations may prove to be — of E. S. Fiorenza, *In Memory of Her*, especially the moving and profoundly true affirmations of pp.343-51. See also the challenging paper of C. Halkes, 'Mary and Women', in H. Küng and J. Moltmann (eds.), *Mary in the Churches*, pp.66-73.

118

⁹⁸ J. M. Robinson (ed.), *The Nag Hammadi Library in English*, p.130. For a discussion of the position of women in the gnostic systems, see K. Rudolph, *Gnosis. The Nature and History of an Ancient Religion*, pp.270-272. See, for further indications to the background for such a change of attitude in the Mary Magdalene - Peter relationship, E. S. Fiorenza, *In Memory of Her*, pp.50-51.

⁹⁹ E. S. Fiorenza, *In Memory of Her*, p. 154. The term 'discipleship of equals' is found throughout this fine book. As I have already suggested, I believe that we have to make this journey towards 'a discipleship of equals' *together*. This is a further feature of the article of J. L. McKenzie, 'The Mother of Jesus in the New Testament', which leaves me unhappy. As he closes his article he suggests that male scholars leave the study of Mary to women, as Paul's dream of Gal. 3,28 is an impossible dream. McKenzie therefore concludes: 'A respect for reality demands that for some time to come we leave Mary in the hands of her sisters. I do not know whether she will be in better hands than in the hands of men; obviously women think so, and the men who created the plaster doll of the traditional Mary should not hesitate to step aside' (p. 10). I disagree, and I hope that, male though I am, I have not 'created a plaster doll of the traditional Mary'.

¹⁰⁰ Rosemary R. Ruether, *Sexism and God-Talk*, p.88, states this case very negatively, situating the whole issue within the very structure of every created reality: 'We alone can "sin". We alone can disrupt and distort the balance of nature and force the price for this distortion on less fortunate humans, as well as the nonhuman community. We cannot do this forever. Finally, the universe will create inversions, under the weight of human distortion and oppression, that will undermine the whole human life-support system. But we may be able to bring the earth down with us in our downfall . . . We are the rogue elephant of nature.' For a more positive statement, see P. Perkins, 'In Jesus' time, women's faithbuilding role vital', *National Catholic Reporter* 20 (No. 25: April 13 1984) pp.16-17. On this, see my own reflections on pp.4-5.

BIBLIOGRAPHY
OF WORKS CITED

AA. VV., *Signs: Journal of Women in Culture and Society* 1- (1975-).

AA. VV., 'The Voices of Women', *Chicago Studies* 19 (1980) pp.111-226 (the whole issue).

AA.VV., 'Woman Doing Theology', *National Catholic Reporter* 20 (No. 25: April 13, 1984).

Agudo, P., 'Intimacy with Self versus self-alienation', in A Polcino (ed.), *Intimacy: Issues of Emotional Living in an Age of Stress for Clergy and Religious* (Whitinsville, Mass., Affirmation Books, 1978) pp.15-23.

Alfaro, J., 'The Mariology of the Fourth Gospel. Mary and the Struggles for Liberation', *Biblical Theology Bulletin* 10 (1980) pp.3-16.

Alter, R., *The Art of Biblical Narrative* (New York, Basic Books, 1981).

Anderson, H., *The Gospel of Mark*, New Century Bible (London, Oliphants, 1976).

Anderson, J. C., 'Matthew: Gender and Reading', *Semeia* 28 (1983) pp.3-27.

Barclay, W., *The Gospels and Acts* (London, SCM Press, 1976) 2 vols.

Barrett, C. K., *The First Epistle to the Corinthians*, Black's New Testament Commentaries (London, A. & C. Black, 1971[2]).

Bearsley, P., 'Mary the Perfect Disciple: a Paradigm for Mariology', *Theological Studies* 41 (1980) pp.461-504.

Beasley, G. R., *The Book of Revelation*, New Century Bible (London, Oliphants, 1978).

Blank, J., 'Frauen in den Jesusüberlieferungen', in G. Dautzenberg *et al.*, *Die Frau im Urchristentum*, pp.9-91.

Bode, E. L., *The First Easter Morning. The Gospel Accounts of the Women's Visit to the Tomb of Jesus*, Analecta Biblica 45 (Rome, Biblical Institute Press, 1970).

Boulding, M., *The Coming of God* (London, SPCK, 1982).

Brennan, I., 'Women in the Gospel', *New Blackfriars* 52 (1971) pp.291-9.

Bryson, R., *The Ministry of Women in the Early Church* (Minnesota, The Liturgical Press, 1976).

Brown, R. E., *The Birth of the Messiah. A Commentary on the Infancy Narratives in Matthew and Luke* (London, Geoffrey Chapman, 1977).

——*The Critical Meaning of the Bible* (London, Geoffrey Chapman, 1981).

——*The Epistles of John*, Anchor Bible 30 (New York, Doubleday, 1982).

——*The Gospel According to John*, Anchor Bible 29-29a (New York, Doubleday, 1966-70) 2 vols.

——'The Meaning of Modern New Testament Studies for an Ecumenical Understanding of Mary', in *Biblical Reflections on Crises Facing the Church* (London, Darton, Longman & Todd, 1975) pp.84-108.

——'The "Mother of Jesus" in the Fourth Gospel', in M. de Jonge (ed.), *L'Evangile de Jean: Sources, rédaction, théologie*, Bibliotheca Ephemeridum Theologicarum Lovaniensium 44 (Gembloux, Duculot, 1977) pp.307-10.

——'The Relation of "The Secret Gospel of Mark" to the Fourth Gospel', *The Catholic Biblical Quarterly* 36 (1974) pp.466-85.

——'Roles of Women in the Fourth Gospel', *Theological Studies* 36 (1975) 688-99. Reprinted in *The Community of the Beloved Disciple* (London, Geoffrey Chapman, 1979) pp.183-98.

——*The Virgin Birth and the Bodily Resurrection of Jesus* (London, Geoffrey Chapman, 1973).

——Donfried, K. P., Fitzmyer, J. A. and Reumann, J. (eds.), *Mary in the New Testament. A Collaborative Assessment by Protestant and Roman Catholic Scholars* (London, Geoffrey Chapman, 1978).

Brütsch, C., *La Clarté de l'Apocalypse* (Geneva, Labor et Fides, 1966[5]).

Bryson, R., *The Ministry of Women in the Early Church* (Minnesota, The Liturgical Press, 1976).

Byrne, B., *'Sons of God — Seed of Abraham'. A Study of the Sonship of God of all Christians in Paul against the Jewish Background*, Analecta Biblica 83 (Rome, Biblical Institute Press, 1979).

Caird, G. B., *St Luke*, Pelican New Testament Commentaries (Harmondsworth, Penguin Books, 1963).

Catholic Biblical Association of America Task Force, 'Women and Priestly Ministry', *The Catholic Biblical Quarterly* 41 (1979) pp.608-13.

Cleary, F. X., 'Women in the New Testament: St. Paul and the Early Pauline Churches', *Biblical Theology Bulletin* 10 (1980) pp.78-82.

Cope, L., 'I Cor. 11,2-16: One Step Further', *Journal for Biblical Literature* 97 (1978) pp.435-6.

Corsini, E., *The Apocalypse. The Perennial Revelation of Jesus Christ*. Good News Studies 5 (Wilmington, Michael Glazier, 1983). Translated and edited by Francis J. Moloney.

Court, H. M., *Myth and History in the Book of Revelation* (London, SPCK, 1979).

Dalton, W., *Mary in the New Testament* (Melbourne, Spectrum, 1974).

Daly, M., *Beyond God the Father: Towards a Philosophy of Women's Liberation* (Boston, Beacon Press, 1973).

Dautzenberg, G., 'Zur Stellung der Frauen in den paulinischen Gemeinden', in G. Dautzenberg *et al.*, *Die Frau im Urchristentum*, pp.182-224.

Dautzenberg, G., Merklein, H. and Müller, K. (eds.), *Die Frau im Urchristentum*, Quaestiones Disputatae 95 (Frieburg/Basel/Wien, Herder, 1983).

Feuillet, A., 'La dignité et le rôle de la femme d'après quelques textes pauliniennes', *New Testament Studies* 21 (1974-75) pp.157-91.

——'The Hour of Jesus and the Sign of Cana', in *Johannine Studies* (Staten Island, Alba House, 1964) pp.17-37.

——*Jèsus et sa Mère d'aprés les rècits lucaniens de l'enfance et d'après Saint Jean. Le rôle de la Vierge Marie dans l'histoire du salut et la place de la femme dans l'église* (Paris, Gabalda, 1974).

Fiorenza, E. S., *In Memory of Her. A Feminist Reconstruction of Christian Origins* (London, SCM Press, 1983).

Fiorenza, E. S. et al. (eds), *The Journal of Feminist Studies in Religion* 1- (1984-).

Fischer, C. — Gatlin, R., *Woman: A Theological Perspective* (Berkeley, Graduate Theological Union, 1974-75).

Fitzmyer, J. A., 'The Priority of Mark and the "Q" Source in Luke', in *To Advance the Gospel. New Testament Studies* (New York, Crossroad, 1981) pp.3-40.

Flanagan, N. M. and Snyder, E. H., 'Did Paul put down women in I Cor. 13,34-36?', *Biblical Theology Bulletin* 11 (1981) pp.10-12.

Georgen, D., *The Sexual Celibate* (New York, Seabury Press, 1974).

Graef, H., *Mary: A History of Doctrine and Devotion* (London, Sheed & Ward, 1963-65) 2 vols.

Greenberg, M., 'Crimes and Punishments', in *the Interpreter's Dictionary of the Bible* (Nashville/New York, Abingdon, 1962) vol. 1, pp.733-44.

Halkes, C., 'Mary and Women', in H. Küng and J. Moltmann (eds.), *Mary in the Churches* (Concilium 168: Edinburgh, T. & T. Clark, 1983) pp.66-73.

Hellwig, M., *Jesus, The Compassion of God. New Perspectives on the Tradition of Christianity*, Theology and Life 9 (Wilmington, Michael Glazier, 1983).

Holtz, T., *Die Christologie der Apocalypse des Johannes*, Texte and Untersuchungen 85 (Akademie Verlag, 1971²).

Hooker, M. D., 'Authority on Her Head: An Examination of I Cor. XI, 10, *New Testament Studies* 10 (1963-64) pp.410-16.

Horton, A., *The Child Jesus* (London, Geoffrey Chapman, 1975).

Hoskyns, E. C. and Davey, F. N. (eds.), *The Fourth Gospel* (London, Faber & Faber, 1947).

Jeremias, J., *Jerusalem, in the Time of Jesus. An Investigation into Economic and Social Conditions during the New Testament Period* (London, SCM Press, 1969).

——*The Parables of Jesus* (London, SCM Press, 1972).

Kenny, J. P., *The Meaning of Mary for Modern Man* (Melbourne, Spectrum, 1980).

Koester, H., *Introduction to the New Testament* (Philadelphia, Fortress Press, 1982) 2 vols.

Kraemer, R. S., 'Women in the Religions of the Greco-Roman World', *Religious Studies Review* 9 (1983) pp.127-39.

Küng, H. and Moltmann, J. (eds.), *Mary in the Churches* (Concilium 168: Edinburgh, T. & T. Clark, 1983).

Lagrange, M. J., *Evangile selon Saint Marc* (Paris, Gabalda, 1920).

LaVerdiere, E. A. and Thompson, W. G., 'New Testament Communities in Transition: A Study in Matthew and Luke', *Theological Studies* 37 (1976) pp.567-97.

Lohfink, G., 'Weibliche Diakone im Neuen Testament', in G. Dautzenberg *et al., Die Frau im Urchristentum*, pp.320-38.

McHugh, J., *The Mother of Jesus in the New Testament* (London, Darton, Longman & Todd, 1975).

McKenzie, J. L., 'The Mother of Jesus in the New Testament', in H. Küng and J. Moltmann (eds.), *Mary in the Churches*, pp.3-11.

Mahoney, R., 'Die Mutter Jesu im Neuen Testament,' in G. Dautzenberg *et al., Die Frau im Urchristentum*, pp.103-10.

Malbon, E. S., 'Fallible Followers: Women and Men in Gospel of Mark', *Semeia* 28 (1983) pp.29-48.

Maly, E. H., 'Women and the Gospel of Luke', *Biblical Theology Bulletin* 10 (1980) pp.99-104.

Marshall, I. H., *The Gospel of Luke. A Commentary on the Greek Text*, The New International Greek Testament and Commentary (Exeter, Paternoster Press, 1978).

——*Luke: Historian and Theologian* (Exeter, Paternoster Press, 1970).

Meier, J. P., *The Vision of Matthew* (New York, Paulist Press, 1979).

Metzger, B. M., *A Textual Commentary on the Greek New Testament* (London/New York, United Bible Societies, 1971).

Moloney, F. J., *Disciples and Prophets. A Biblical Model for the Religious Life* (London, Darton, Longman & Todd, 1980).

——'Faith in the Risen Jesus', *Salesianum* 43 (1981) pp.305-16.

——'From Cana to Cana (Jn 2,1-4,54) and the Fourth Evangelist's Concept of Correct (and Incorrect) Faith', in E. A. Livingston (ed.), *Studia Biblica II. Papers on the Gospels. Sixth International Congress on Biblical Studies. Oxford 3-7 April 1978*, JSNT Supplement Series 2 (Sheffield, JSOT Press, 1980). Also available in *Salesianum* 40 (1978) pp.817-43.

——'The Infancy Narratives. Another View of Raymond Brown's "The Birth of the Messiah" ', *The Clergy Review* 64 (1979) pp.161-6.

——'The Johannine Son of God', *Salesianum* 38 (1976) pp.71-86.

——*The Johannine Son of Man*, Biblioteca di Scienze Religiose 14 (Rome, Libreria Ateneo Salesiano, 1978²).

——'John 17: The Prayer of Jesus' Hour', *The Clergy Review* 67 (1982) pp.79-83.

——'John 20: A Journey Completed', *The Australasian Catholic Record* 59 (1982) pp.417-32.

——*A Life of Promise: Poverty, Chastity, Obedience*, Consecrated Life Series 1 (Wilmington, Michael Glazier, 1984).

——*Mary: A Gospel Portrait* (Melbourne, St Paul's Audio Visuals, 1982) 3 Cassettes.

——'Matthew 19,3-13 and Celibacy. A Form Critical and Redaction Critical Study', *Journal for the Study of the New Testament* 2 (1979) pp.42-60.

——'The Vocation of the Disciples in the Gospel of Mark', *Salesianum* 43 (1981) pp.487-516.

Moltmann-Wendel, E., *The Women around Jesus. Reflections on Authentic Personhood* (London, SCM Press, 1982).
'Motherhood or Friendship', in H. Küng and J. Moltmann (eds.) *Mary in the Churches*, pp.17-22.

Mortley, R., *Womanhood. The Feminine in Ancient Hellenism, Gnosticism, Christianity and Islam* (Sydney, Delacroix, 1981).

Munro, W., 'Women Disciples in Mark?', *The Catholic Biblical Quarterly* 44 (1982) pp.225-41.

Murphy-O'Connor, J., *Becoming Human Together. The Pastoral Anthropology of St. Paul*, Good News Studies 2 (Wilmington, Michael Glazier, 1982²).

——*I Corinthians*, New Testament Message 10 (Wilmington, Michael Glazier, 1979).

——'The Non-Pauline Character of I Corinthians 11,2-16', *Journal for Biblical Literature* 95 (1976) pp.615-21.

——'Sex and Logic in I Corinthians 11,2-16', *The Catholic Biblical Quarterly* 42 (1980) pp.482-500.

O'Carroll, M., *Theotokos. A Theological Encyclopedia of the Blessed Virgin Mary* (Wilmington, Michael Glazier, 1983²).

Perkins, P., 'In Jesus' time, women's faith building role vital', *National Catholic Reporter* 20 (No. 25: April 13 1984) pp.16-17.

Pesch, R., *Das Markusevangelium*, Herders Theologischer Kommentar zum Neuen Testament 11/1-2 (Freiburg/Basel/Wien, Herder, 1977²).

Phipps, W. E., *The Sexuality of Jesus* (New York, Harper & Row, 1973).

Priestley, D., *Bringing Forth in Hope. Being Creative in a Nuclear Age* (New York, Paulist Press, 1983).

Quesnell, Q., 'The Mar Saba Clementine: A Question of Evidence', *The Catholic Biblical Quarterly* 37 (1975) pp.48-67.

——'The Women at Luke's Supper', in R. J. Cassidy and P. J. Scharper (eds.), *Political Issues in Luke-Acts* (New York, Orbis Books, 1983) pp.59-79.

Rees, D. and others, *Consider Your Call. A Theology of Monastic Life Today* (London, SPCK, 1978).

Ritt, H., 'Die Frauen und die Osterbotschaft. Synopse der Grabesgeschichten (Mk 16,1-8; Mt 27,62-28,15; Lk 24,1-2; Joh 20, 1-18)', in G. Dautzenberg *et al., Die Frau im Urchristentum*, pp. 117-33.

Robinson, J. M. (ed.)., *The Nag Hammadi Library in English* (Leiden, E. J. Brill, 1977).

Ross, M., *The Fire of Your Life. A Solitude Shared* (New York, Paulist Press, 1983).

Rudolph, K., *Gnosis. The Nature and History of an Ancient Religion* (Edinburgh T. & T. Clark, 1983).

Ruether, R. R., *Sexism and God-Talk. Towards a Feminist Theology* (London, SCM Press, 1983).

Sayers, D. L., *Unpopular Opinions* (London, Victor Gollancz, 1946).

Schnackenburg, R., *The Gospel according to St John* (London, Burns & Oates/New York, Crossroad, 1968-1982) 3 vols.

Schelkle, K.-H., *The Spirit and the Bride: Woman in the Bible* (Collegeville, Liturgical Press, 1977).

Schmitt, J., 'Women in Mark's Gospel', *The Bible Today* 19 (1981) pp.228-33.

Schneiders, S. M., 'The Effects of Women's Experience on Their Spirituality', *Spirituality Today* 35 (1983) pp.100-16.

——'Women in the Fourth Gospel and the Role of Women in the Contemporary Church', *Biblical Theology Bulletin* 12 (1982) pp.35-45.

Schweizer, E., *The Good News according to Matthew* (London, SPCK, 1976).

Scroggs, R., 'Paul and the Eschatological Woman', *Journal for the American Academy of Religion* 40 (1972) pp.283-303.

——'Paul and the Eschatological Woman: Revisited', *Journal for the American Academy of Religion* 42 (1974) pp.532-7.

——'Paul: Chauvinist or Liberationist?' *The Christian Century* 89 (1972) pp.307-9.

Segovia, F. F., *Love Relationships in the Johannine Tradition: Agapē/Agapan in I John and the Fourth Gospel*, SBL Dissertation Series 58 (Chico, Scholars Press, 1982).

Senior, D., *What are they saying about Matthew?* (New York, Paulist Press, 1983).

Simoens, Y., *La gloire d'aimer. Structures stylistiques et interprétatives dans le Discours de la Cène*, Analecta 90 (Rome, Biblical Institute Press, 1981).

Smith, M., *The Secret Gospel. The Discovery and Interpretation of the Secret Gospel According to Mark* (London, Victor Gollancz, 1974).

Stagg, E. and Stagg, F., *Woman in the World of Jesus*, (Edinburgh, The Saint Andrew Press, 1978).

Stockton, E., 'The Fourth Gospel and the Woman', in N. Brown (ed.), *Essays in Faith and Culture* (Sydney, Catholic Institute of Sydney, 1979) pp.132-44.

Strack, H. L. and Billerbeck, P., *Kommentar zum Neuen Testament aus Talmud und Midrasch* (München, C. H. Beck, 1926-61) 6 vols.

Taylor, V., *The Gospel According to St Mark*(London, Macmillan, 1966²).

——*The Passion Narrative of St Luke. A Critical and Historical Investigation*, SNTS Monograph Series 19 (Cambridge, University Press, 1972).

Tavard, G. H., *Woman in Christian Tradition* (Indiana, University of Notre Dame Press, 1973).

Tetlow, E. M., *Women and Ministry in the New Testament* (New York, Paulist Press, 1980).

Tolbert, M. A., 'Defining the Problem: The Bible and Feminist Hermeneutics', *Semeia* 28 (1983) pp.113-26.

Trompf, G. W., 'On Attitudes toward Women in Paul and Paulinist Literature', *The Catholic Biblical Quarterly* 42 (1980) pp.196-215.

Vawter, B., *On Genesis. A New Reading* (New York, Doubleday, 1977).

von Campenhausen, H., 'The Events of Easter and the Empty Tomb', in *Tradition and Life in the Church. Essays and Lectures in Church History* (London, Collins, 1968) pp.42-89.

von Rad, G., *Genesis. A Commentary* (London, SCM Press, 1963).

Wahlberg, R. C., *Jesus According to a Woman* (New York, Paulist Press, 1975).

Walker, W. O., 'I Cor. 11,2-16 and Paul's Views Regarding Women', *Journal for Biblical Literature* 94 (1975) pp.94-110.

——'The "Theology of Woman's Place" and the "Paulinist" Tradition', *Semeia* 28 (1983) pp.101-12.